The Golden Palace

The Ultimate Viewing Guide

Harry R. Huryk

The Golden Palace

This book is dedicated to my grandfather, Robert Carswell. Through my entire life his thoughts and feelings on life and the world around us have helped to truly inspire me. Now, well into his later years, my grandfather has found the inspiration in himself to become an author. I can think of no other person in the world who I am more proud to share the hobby of writing with than my "Pop Pop."

Thank you very much for always inspiring me and believing in me. You will be an enormous part of my world as long as I live.

Love,

Table of Contents

-Preface-

The Golden Palace was an interesting show in the world of television spin-offs, primarily because it utilized almost the entire cast of the original show. When Bea Arthur announced her departure from *The Golden Girls,* the creators decided to move the show into a different territory. The characters moved to an entire new set with two new main characters joining the lineup. Now, the three remaining girls were joined by Don Cheadle as Roland and Cheech Marin as Chuy. Another character, Oliver, shows up as Roland's foster child. Although Oliver, played by Billy Sullivan, plays a character who should seemingly be in almost every episode, we only see him in a total of seven. Eventually, Oliver would be reunited with his mother, leaving the series completely.

The show followed the continuing trials and tribulations of the five main characters attempting to run a successful hotel in the swanky Miami Beach. Almost every episode focused at least partly on issues with the hotel itself and the methods the characters used to solve those issues.

This guide was created to be a tribute to the show. While the series was short lived, I have always considered *The Golden Palace* to be an eighth season of *The Golden Girls.* After having created The Golden Girls – The Ultimate Viewing Guide, I saw the need to finish the collection by creating this book. While this book is admittedly shorter, it is still the most informative guide to *The Golden Palace.*

In this book, you'll find a full episode guide, highlighting the guest stars, the title, and a full description of each episode. Use the guide as a reference to compare episodes to each other and find your favorites! You'll also find a "Goofs, Notes and Observations" section of the book. There, you'll enjoy little tidbits and issues about each episode. Couple these sections with actor and actress work biographies and histories of the characters, plus a trivia section and you've got a great guide to a great show.

The Golden Palace may have been short lived, and if it was any other show it would have been long forgotten. But, with an unforgettable cast, great writing and directly following the story line of *The Golden Girls, The Golden Palace* was a winner. Enjoy this book and use it as a chance to find more love for those crazy ladies from Miami who always were, and will always be, our golden girls.

Harry R. Huryk

Please Meet: Estelle Getty!

Character on The Golden Palace: Sophia Petrillo

Date of Birth: July 25, 1923 (New York City, N.Y.)

Date of Death: July 22, 2008 (Los Angeles, CA)

Estelle was born in 1923 in New York City to parents Sarah and Charles Scher, Jewish immigrants from Poland. Her parents worked in the glass industry. As Estelle grew, she began to find enjoyment in Yiddish theatre and Broadway stage productions.

Estelle found her first start in the performing business in some of these Yiddish theatres and also as a comedienne in the Catskills Borscht Belt Resorts. Later, she would find the role of Harvey Fierstein's mother in the Broadway production of *Torch Song Trilogy.* Her career on and off Broadway brought her many roles and moderate success.

In the mid 1980's, Estelle decided to set her sights on a television spot. During her final call-back for what would eventually become the role of Sophia Petrillo, the producers were uneasy about her nervousness. But, as we all know, Estelle would prevail and would eventually become the most famous Italian mother on television. The role of Sophia seemed to have been made for Estelle, and she played it with amazing talent.

Further capitalizing on her Hollywood fame, Estelle would write a book about her life titled *If I Knew Then What I Know Now…So What?* Seeing the need to keep senior citizens in better health, she also released an exercise video in 1993.

Estelle was married to Arthur Gettleman from 1947 through his death in 2004. The stage name "Getty" was adapted from her married name. Getty believed the shorter name sounded more "Hollywood." Arthur and Estelle had two children, Carl and Barry.

In 1991, Getty helped a nephew who was stricken with AIDS. The nephew's parents lived in England, and the young man in North Carolina. Estelle had the failing relative flown to California and set up hospice for his final days. Her nephew died in January 1992. Witnessing the devastation AIDS can have, Estelle set out to educate the world on the disease. She would also fight for the rights of gays and lesbians.

In 2000 Getty stopped making public appearances altogether, revealing that she had Parkinson's disease and an advanced case of Osteoporosis. A few years later, media reports would also state that she was suffering from Alzheimer's. However, doctors would later discover that she had neither Parkinson's nor Alzheimer's. It turns out, Getty was actually suffering from Lewy body dementia.

Lifetime Television would eventually run a reunion show for *The Golden Girls*. However, due to quickly declining health, Estelle would not be able to attend. The other three cast members did an amazing job remembering Getty and her unforgettable character on the show.

Estelle passed away on July 22, 20008 at approximately 5:30AM. She passed away just days before what would have been her 85th birthday. Hollywood mourned the loss of Estelle as one of the most talented actresses of our time. Her three most famous co-stars all reflected on their life with Estelle.

SPOTLIGHT ON: Estelle Getty

Production Name:	Year	Character
Team-Mates	1978	Teacher
Tootsie	1982	Middle-Aged Woman
Deadly Force	1983	Gussie
Fantasy Island	1984	Money Lady
Cagney and Lacey	1984	Mrs. Rosenmeyer
No Man's Land	1984	Eurol Muller
Hotel	1984	Roberta
Victims for Victims: The Theresa Saldana Story	1984	
Mask	1985	Evelyn
Newhart	1985	Miriam the Librarian
Copacabana	1985	Bella Stern
Mannequin	1987	Claire Prince Timkin
City	1990	Helen Rutledge
Blossom	1991	Sophia Petrillo
Empty Nest	1988-95	Sophia Petrillo
Stop! Or My Mom Will Shoot!	1992	Tutti Bomowski
The Golden Girls	1985-92	Sophia Petrillo
The Golden Palace	1992-93	Sophia Petrillo
Nurses	1993	Sophia Petrillo

Production Name:	Year	Character
Touched By An Angel	1996	Dottie
Brotherly Love	1996	Myrna
A Match Made In Heaven	1997	Betty Weston
Mad About You	1997	Paul's Aunt
Duckman: Private Dick/Family Man	1997	Aunt Jane
The Sissy Duckling	1999	Mrs. Hennypecker
Staurt Little	1999	Grandma Estelle Little
The Million Dollar Kid	2000	Sister Rosanne
Ladies Man	2000	Sophia Gates

Please Meet: Rue McClanahan!

Character on The Golden Palace: Blanche Devereaux

Date of Birth: February 21, 1934 (Healdton, OK)

Rue McClanahan was born Eddi Rue McClanahan on February 21, 1934 in Healdton, Oklahoma. Her parents were Dreda Rheua-Nell, a professional beautician, and William Edwin McClanahan, a building construction contractor. Rue is of Choctaw Indian and Irish ancestry. She grew up in the town of Ardmore, Oklahoma and graduated from the local high school in 1953. She attended the University of Tulsa, majoring in German language and performing theatre. While in college, she was an active member of the sorority Kappa Alpha Theta.

Rue began her acting career in the off-Broadway circuit in 1957. Finally in 1969, she made her Broadway debut portraying Sally Weber in the original production of the musical *Jimmy Shine*. Rue found her first official "breakout role" with a run on *Another World* as nanny Caroline Johnson. The role lasted from July 1970 to September 1971. Even though the role was negative in nature, Rue found many fans in the world of daytime television. Eventually, she would land another role on the show *Where the Heart Is*, portraying Margaret Jordan.

McClanahan appeared in various productions such as *The Rotten Apple* and *Walk the Angry Beach*. In 1971, she played a vicious character in the film *Some of My Best Friends Are…* which was set in a shabby 1970's gay bar. Rue also took on the challenging role of an Al-Anon leader in a video entitled "Slight Drinking Problem." Eventually, Rue would begin acting on *Mama's Family* as Aunt Fran Crowley from 1983 to 1985. Here, she would work with eventual co-star of *The Golden Girls*, Betty White.

On The Golden Girls, we saw Rue fit very nicely into the role of Blanche Devereaux. Blanche's sex-obsessed escapades made her a very unusual, yet loveable character. The story line showed Blanche as the owner of a house the four stars lived in. A widow, Blanche needed to take in some boarders, and as such, the world of *The Golden Girls* was born. Of course, following the close of the show, Rue, Estelle and Betty would continue onto new roles in the spin-off *The Golden Palace*. After just one season, *The Golden Palace* was cancelled due to lackluster ratings.

Rue is an active advocate of People for the Ethical Treatment of Animals (PETA) and is a supporter of the Democratic Party. Rue is said to have had written a letter to John Kerry insisting that she was refusing to vote for him due to his hunting activities. She did vote for Barack Obama in 2008.

Rue was diagnosed with breast cancer in June of 1997. She fought and survived the disease. She has since attended rallies and events for the support of breast cancer research.

Rue released a book in the spring of 2007, titled <u>My First Five Husbands and the Ones Who Got Away.</u> Rue is currently married to Morrow Wilson, her sixth marriage. Her other five husbands are Tom Bish, Norman Hartweg, Peter DMaior, Gus Fisher, and Tom Keel. From all of these marriages, she only ended up with one child.

Rue continues to work, even though she is well into her eighties. As long as she is able to, she states she will continue to work in Hollywood. Rue has a career that spans into film, television and theatre. She continues to live and work in Hollywood and advances her career anytime she can.

SPOTLIGHT ON: Rue McClanahan

Production Name:	Year	Character
The Grass Eater	1961	Loraina
Door to Door Maniac	1961	Pamela
Five Minutes to Love	1963	Sally 'Poochie'
How to Suceed with Girls	1964	
Burke's Law	1964	Waitress
Angel's Flight	1965	Dolly
Walk the Angry Beach	1968	Sandy
The People Next Door	1970	Della
Another World	1964	Caroline Johnson
The Pursuit of Happiness	1971	Mrs. O'Mara
They Might Be Giants	1971	Daisy Playfair
Hogan's Goat	1971	Josey Finn
Some of My Best Friends Are	1971	Lita Joyce
Where the Heart Is	1971-1972	Margaret Jardin
Love of Life	1971	Mrs. Braylee
All in the Family	1972	Ruth Rempley
ABC Afternoon Playbreak	1973	Carol Babcock
Blade	1973	Gail
The Rimers of Eldritch	1974	Cora Groves
Mannix	1974	

Production Name:	Year	Character
Insight	1975-1977	Linda
Maude	1972-1977	Vivian
A Different Approach	1978	
Having Babies III	1978	Gloria Miles
Sergeant Matlovich vs. The U.S. Air Force	1978	Mat's Mom
Grandpa Goes to Washington	1978	Grace
Apple Pie	1978	Ginger-Nell Hollyhock
Rainbow	1978	Ida Koverman
Supertrain	1979	Janet
Topper	1979	Clara Topper
Lou Grant	1980	Maggie McKenna
Here's Boomer	1980	Thelma
Gridlock	1980	Adele Sherman
Word of Honor	1981	Maggie McNeil
And They Lived Happily Ever After	1981	Liz Wescott
Darkroom	1981	Mrs. Louise Michaelson
The Day the Bubble Burst	1982	Barbara Avery
Trapper John M.D.	1982	Mary
Fantasy Island	1979-1982	Gertie
Newhart	1983	Eleanor Smathers
The Skin of Our Teeth	1983	Fortune Teller
Small and Frye	1983	Miss Parsifal
Mama's Family	1983-1985	Aunt Fran Crowley
Gimme A Break!	1981-1984	Katrina

Production Name:	Year	Character
Alice	1984	Mother Goose
The Love Boat	1978-1984	Mary Hubble
Cover Up	1984	Mattie Bemstein
Crazy Like a Fox	1985	
Charles in Charge	1984-1985	Grandma Irene
Murder, She Wrote	1985	Miriam Radford
Picnic	1986	Flo Owens
The Little Match Girl	1987	Frances Dutton
Liberace	1988	Frances Liberace
Empty Nest	1988	Blanche Devereaux
Take My Daughters, Please	1988	Lilah Page
The Man in the Brown Suit	1989	Suzy Blair
Nightmare Classics	1989	
The Wickedest Witch	1989	Avarissa
American Playrights - The One Acts	1990	Miss Moray
Modern Love	1990	Mrs. Evelyn Parker
After the Shock	1990	Sherra Cox
Children of the Bride	1990	Margaret Becker
To My Daughter	1990	Laura Carlson
The Dreamer of Oz	1990	Matilda Electra Joslyn Gage
Biosphere 2	1991	Hostess
Baby of the Bride	1991	Margaret Hix
Nurses	1992	Blanche Devereaux
The Golden Girls	1985-1992	Blanche Devereaux

Production Name:	Year	Character
Nunsense	1993	Mother Mary Regina
Mother of the Bride	1993	Margaret Becker Hix
The Golden Palace	1992-1993	Blanche Devereaux
Message From Nam	1993	Beatrice Andrews
Boy Meets World	1993	Bernice Matthews
Nunsense 2: The Sequel	1994	Mother Superior Sister Mary Regina
Days Like This	1994	Glenda
Burke's Law	1994	Jinxy Duke
A Burning Passion: Margaret Mitchell Story	1994	Grandma Stephens
Blackbird Hall	1995	
The Mommies	1995	Amanda Kellogg
Spider Man	1995	Anastasia Hardy
A Holiday to Remember	1995	Miz Leona
Innocent Victims	1996	Marylou Hennis
Dear God	1996	Mom Turner
Remember WENN	1996	Dusty Foxx
Dads	1997	Dr. Neuhauser
This World, Then the Fireworks	1997	Mom Lakewood
Promised Land	1997	Valerie Carter
Murphy Brown	1997	Virginia Redfield
Out to Sea	1997	Ellen Carruthers
Annabelle's Wish	1997	Scarlett
Starship Troopers	1997	Biology Teacher

Production Name:	Year	Character
Nunsense Jamboree	1998	Mother Superior Sister Mary Regina
Border to Border	1998	Mrs. Kirby
Rusty: A Dog's Tale	1998	Edna Callahan
Columbo: Ashes to Ashes	1998	Verity Chandler
The Love Boat: The Next Wave	1998	Abigail Jordan
A Saintly Switch	1999	Aunt Fanny
Blue's Clues	1999	Steve's Grandmother
Blue's Big Treasure Hunt	1999	Grandma
Safe Harbor	1999	Grandma Loring
The Lot	1999	Priscilla Tremaine
Ladies Man	2000	Aunt Lou
The Moving of Sophia Myles	2000	Mary-Margaret
Touched by an Angel	1994-2001	Lila Winslow
Nuncrackers	2001	Reverand Mother
Stage on Screen: The Women	2002	Countless DeLage
Miracle Dogs	2003	Katherine Mannion
The Fighting Temptations	2003	Nancy Stringer
Wonderfalls	2004	Millie Marcus
Whoopi	2004	Marian
Wit's End	2005	Dean Madison
Hope and Faith	2005	Sylvia
Back To You and Me	2005	Helen Ludwick
King of the Hill	2007	Bunny
Sordid Lives: The Series	2008	Peggy Ingram

Please Meet: Betty White!

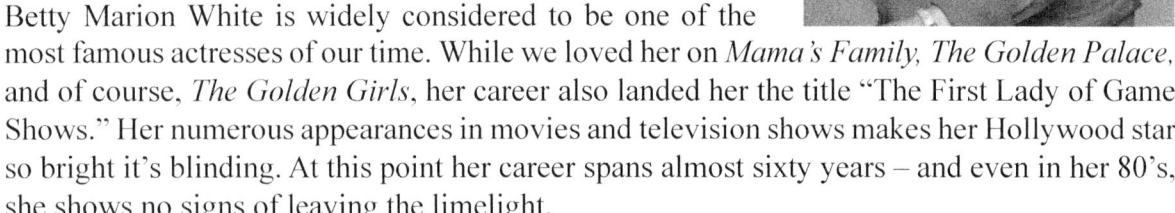

Character on The Golden Palace: Rose Nylund

Date of Birth: January 17, 1922 (Oak Park, IL)

Betty Marion White is widely considered to be one of the most famous actresses of our time. While we loved her on *Mama's Family, The Golden Palace,* and of course, *The Golden Girls,* her career also landed her the title "The First Lady of Game Shows." Her numerous appearances in movies and television shows makes her Hollywood star so bright it's blinding. At this point her career spans almost sixty years – and even in her 80's, she shows no signs of leaving the limelight.

Betty was born on January 17, 1922 in Oak Park, Illinois. She is the daughter of Horace L. White, a traveling salesman and his wife Tess. She has German and Greek heritage. She was raised in Los Angeles, CA and attended Horace Mann Middle School and Beverly Hills High. She graduated in 1939.

Before she began her television career, Betty began working as a model. However, it wasn't too long before she found the role of Elizabeth on the show *Life with Elizabeth* from 1953 to 1955. The show found her the first Emmy nomination of her career. She then went on to play Vicki Angel on the show *Date with the Angels* from 1957 to 1958. In 1954, she also hosted a talk show for a short time entitled *The Betty White Show.* Betty also ended up doing several radio and television commercials in the Los Angeles area.

From 1961 to 1975, Betty made several appearances on the largely popular game show *Password.* White would eventually marry the show's host, Allen Ludden in 1963. She also made several, sometimes frequent, appearances on other game shows such as *Password, Super Password,* and *Million Dollar Password.* In 1983, Betty became the first woman to win a daytime Emmy Award for the category of Outstanding Game Show Host for the NBC program *Just Men.*

In 1973, White landed the role of Sue Ann Nivens, "The Happy Homemaker" on *The Mary Tyler Moore Show.* Betty won two Emmy Awards for her portrayal of the character on one of the most popular shows in television history.

In 1977, Betty was given her own sit-com titled *The Betty White Show* on CBS. The cast was rounded out by John Hillerman and former co-star Georgia Engel. Unfortunately, the show was cancelled after just one season.

Betty's most major roles came in the 1980's. Beginning in 1983, she took on the role of Ellen Harper Jackson on the series *Mama's Family.* She stayed with the show for two years and then began the most important role of her career.

On *The Golden Girls,* White was amazing as the constantly naïve, yet always warm-heated, Rose Nylund. Rose was constantly the one who gave bits of wisdom from her home town of St.Olaf, Minnesota. Originally, White was to be cast as Blanche, the character that would eventually belong to Rue McClanahan. But, the producers and directors of the show knew that White was able to handle the constant stream of naïve behavior necessary. Betty won an Emmy for her first year on *The Golden Girls,* and was nominated every year the show ran. After the conclusion of the show in 1992, Betty would continue onto the new spin-off show, *The Golden Palace.* The show only lasted one season before it was cancelled due to lackluster ratings.

White continues her work in Hollywood to this day. Even though she is now in her mid-eighties, she shows no signs of slowing down. Admittedly, she is beginning to show her age, but when you consider all she is involved in, she's truly a remarkable woman. She is involved in several animal protection projects. She also donates time and funds to the Los Angeles Zoo for improvement projects. White is also a spokesperson for 1 800 Pet Meds, an order-by-phone pet pharmacy.

As one of the two remaining characters from *The Golden Girls,* White continues to go strong. While she has had a most remarkable career in almost every corner of Hollywood, it is her immensely strong role of Rose on *The Golden Girls* and The Golden Palace that we will never forgot for years to come.

SPOTLIGHT ON: Betty White

Production Name:	Year	Character
Time to Kill	1945	
Hollywood on Television	1949	Phone Girl
Life with Elizabeth	1953-1955	Elizabeth
The Millionaire	1956	Virginia Lennart
Date with the Angels	1957-1958	Vicki Angel
Advise and Consent	1962	Senator Bessie Adams
The United States Steel Hour	1962	
Petticoat Junction	1969	Adelle Colby
The Pet Set	1971	Hostess
Lucas Tanner	1975	Lydia Merrick
Ellery Queen	1975	Lousie Demery
Mary Tyler Moore	1973-1977	Sue Ann Nivens
The John Davidson Christmas Special	1977	
A Different Approach	1978	
The Betty White Show	1977-1978	
The Carol Burnett Show	1975-1978	(Various Characters)
With this Ring	1978	Evelyn Harris
Snavely	1978	Gladys Snavely
The Best Place to Be	1979	Sally Cantrell
Before and After	1979	Anita

Production Name:	Year	Character
The Gossip Columnist	1980	
Stephanie	1981	Agnes Dewey
Love, Sidney	1982	Charlotte
Best of the West	1982	
Eunice	1982	Ellen
Fame	1983	Catherine
Hotel	1984	
St. Elsewhere	1985	Capt. Gloria Neal
The Love Boat	1980-1985	Betsy
Who's the Boss?	1985	Bobby Barnes
Mama's Family	1983-1986	Ellen Harper Jackson
Alf Loves a Mystery	1987	Aunt Harriet
Santa Barbara	1988	Waitress
Another World	1988	Brenda Barlowe
Carol and Company	1990	Trisha Durant
Nurses	1991	Rose Lindstrom Nylund
Chance of a Lifetime	1991	Evelyn Eglin
Empty Nest	1989-1992	Rose Lindstrom Nylund
The Golden Girls	1985-1992	Rose Lindstrom Nylund
The Golden Palace	1985-1992	Rose Lindstrom Nylund
Bob	1992	Sylvia Schmidt
Diagnosis Murder	1994	Dora
Maybe this Time	1995	Shirley
The Story of Santa Claus	1996	Gretchen Claus

Production Name:	Year	Character
A Weekend in the Country	1996	Martha
Suddenly Susan	1996	Midge Haber
The Lionhearts	1998	Dorothy
Me and George	1998	
Hard Rain	1998	Doreen Sears
Dennis the Menace Strikes Again!	1998	Martha Wilson
L.A. Doctors	1998	Mrs. Brooks
Hercules	1999	Hestia
Lake Placid	1999	Mrs. Delores Bickerman
The Story of Us	1999	Lillian Jordan
Ally McBeal	1999	Dr. Shirley Flott
Tom Sawyer	2000	Aunt Polly
Whispers: An Elephant's Tale	2000	Round
The Wild Thornberrys	2000	Sophie Hunter
The Wild Thornberrys	2000	Grandma Sophie
Ladies Man	1999-2001	Mitzi Stiles
The Retrievers	2001	Mrs. Krisper
The Ellen Show	2001	Connie Gibson
Yes, Dear	2002	Sylvia
Providence	2002	Julianna
Kind of the Hill	1999-2002	Delia
That 70's Show	2002-2003	Bea Sigurdson
Bringing Down the House	2003	Mrs. Kline
Return to the Batcave	2003	Woman in Window

Production Name:	Year	Character
Grim and Evil	2003	Mrs. Doolin
Gary the Rat	2003	Gary's Mother
Stealing Christmas	2003	Emily Sutton
The Practice	2004	Catherine Piper
Everwood	2003-2004	Carol Roberts
My Wife and Kids	2004	June Hopkins
Malcolm in the Middle	2004	Sylvia
Father of the Pride	2004	Grandma Wilson
Annie's Point	2005	Annie Eason
The Third Wish	2005	Lettie
Complete Savages	2004-2005	Mrs. Riley
Joey	2005	Joey and the House
Higglytown Heroes	2004-2007	Grandma
Sea Tales	2007	(voice only)
Gake no ue no Ponyo	2008	(voice only)
The Bold and the Beautiful	2006-2008	Ann Douglas
Boston Legal	2005-2008	Catherine Piper
Love N' Dancing	2009	Irene
My Name is Earl	2009	Mrs. Weezmer
The Proposal	2009	Grandma Annie

PLEASE BE SEATED...I'D LIKE TO INTRODUCE...

Rose Lindstrom - Nylund

Rose Nylund ended up in Miami after spending a majority of her life in the small farming town of St. Olaf, Minnesota. Anyone who has seen even one episode of *The Golden Girls,* or *The Golden Palace* has heard references to the backwards town and the goofy residents who inhabit it. Heavily inhabited by people of Norwegian descent, their levels of intelligence are below normal to say the least.

Rose is the only child of a woman named Ingrid who died during childbirth, and a monk named Martin. After she was born, Rose was adopted by the Lindstrom family who would raise her as their own. Rose ended up with nine siblings, but through the course of the series, we only meet two, Lily and Holly. In her earlier life, she maintained a rather odd fantasy that Bob Hope was her father. But, she eventually meets her actual father while performing candy-striper work at a local hospital.

After a rather interesting upbringing on a dairy farm, Rose would begin to date and eventually marry Charlie Nylund. After marriage, Charlie and Rose have five children – Kristin, Bridget, Charlie Jr., Adam and Janella. After their children were grown, Charlie and Rose continued their lives together until Charlie eventually passed away from a heart attack.

After his passing, Rose could no longer live in the house that was so full of memories of Charlie. After dealing with the grief for quite some time and weighing all the consequences, Rose made the decision to relocate to Miami.

As Rose arrives in Miami, she takes an apartment with a woman who will eventually ask her to leave due to the fact that she has a cat. Rose finds herself in a supermarket, looking at a bulletin board, where she meets Blanche. Soon enough, the four ladies are housemates – the world of *The Golden Girls* has now begun.

Rose takes a job as a grief counselor. However, later in the series, she receives notice that she will no longer be receiving pension checks from a company her late husband worked for. As such, she gets a job as a production assistant with a local consumer reporter. At one point, she does land a job as a reporter, but completely messes up the opportunity. She also lands a job as an associate producer on the local show *Wake Up Miami.*

Through the series Rose has her share of love interests, the most prevalent being Miles, a local college professor. Late in the series we discover that Miles is actually in the witness protection program and his name is actually Nicholas Carbone. However, the mobster who was after

Miles is eventually caught, allowing Miles to continue his relationship with Rose.

As the series closes, we see Rose choosing to stay in Miami with Sophia and Blanche after Dorothy marries and moves out. As we all know, Rose would go on to the new show *The Golden Palace* where the girls run a Miami Beach hotel.

TIMES AT THE GOLDEN PALACE

As an employee of the Golden Palace, we see a slightly different Rose. To begin with, she is seen as more of a leader, with a lot more backbone. This is explained by the fact that she is now one of the co-owners of the hotel. While the St. Olaf stories still creep in from time to time, the references to the crazy town are less frequent. At times, she still displays the severely naïve personality of the Rose from *The Golden Girls* story line. But, this Rose also appears to have a little more of an edge. Constant customer and guest complaints sometimes rub her the wrong way, as do Blanche's attempts to skirt hotel responsibilities.

The Golden Palace shows the end of the Rose and Miles relationship, carried over from *The Golden Girls.* While they are still actively dating at the beginning of the series, Miles is caught seeing another woman. Rose will eventually end their relationship and is, for a time, heartbroken. In a later episode Miles marries another woman at the Golden Palace. After Rose witnesses the wedding, the closure she needs, Miles is removed from the story line completely.

Rose also ends up in new friendships with characters Chuy, Roland and Oliver. Rose and Chuy are hysterical together, with Rose's stories of St. Olaf and Chuy's stories of growing up in East Los Angeles. With Roland, the laughter comes from his attempts to manage the hotel successfully while continually clashing with Rose's mishaps. Of course, the sweet and wonderfulness of Rose is shown with Oliver in her advice to the youngster.

All in all, Rose continues to be Rose, and the character from *The Golden Girls* is not lost. A different Rose, yes, but our favorite former resident of Minnesota is still with us, now running the Golden Palace.

PLEASE BE SEATED...I'D LIKE TO INTRODUCE...

Blanche Hollingsworth - Devereaux

Blanche Hollingsworth grew up in Georgia on a plantation that we assume was located somewhere outside Atlanta. Blanche often makes references to her family life on the plantation. She had two sisters, Charmaine and Virginia and two brothers Clayton and Tad. We had the chance to meet three of her siblings on *The Golden Girls* and each of them brought problems to Blanche when they visited. Of all, the most difficult for Blanche was the admittance from her brother Clayton that he was gay.

Blanche was close with her parents even though she usually drove them crazy with her escapades as a teen. She always referred to her father as "Big Daddy" and in an episode that dealt with his death, we realize how much she really did love him.

As a young woman, Blanche married George Devereaux. The two had six children, Rebecca, Janet, Skippy, Biff, Doug and Matthew. We did meet her son Matthew, and her daughters Janet and Rebecca. She also had several grandchildren. David, Melissa, Aurora and Sarah made appearances on *The Golden Girls.* Her obsession with being viewed as much younger than she actually was lead to problems with her children when they were growing up. Blanche indicates a few times that she didn't enjoy being a mother because it made her appear older.

Blanche and George purchased the famed Golden Girls house in Miami, and continued to live their lives together. When George's untimely death occurred, Blanche needed to take in some boarders to help with the rent. According to one episode, Blanche had other boarders before Rose and Dorothy, described as two older women from Minnesota. However, Blanche didn't get along with them, and soon ended up with Dorothy and Rose. As we all know, the fire at Shady Pines would soon add Sophia, and complete the living situation.

Blanche is shown as being a constantly horny and obsessed with men. She dates a new man in almost every episode, and often ends up hurt when her vanity and indecisions make her back away from guys who are probably good catches. Even though she acts this way, she always insisted that she was extremely faithful to her husband.

Later in the series, we are presented with the fact that her husband George had been un-faithful to her and there is now a son named David. David appears in one episode and meets Blanche. At first, she treats David with extreme anger and contempt, but eventually realizes that David is a part of the only man she ever really loved.

At the close of the series Blanche stays with Rose and Sophia in the house after Dorothy leaves to marry Blanche's Uncle Lucas. After this, the girls decide to buy a Miami Beach hotel, the Golden Palace. To buy the hotel, they sell Blanche's house and move out.

TIMES AT THE GOLDEN PALACE

The character of Blanche on *The Golden Palace* is slightly different, but her personality flaws carry over from *The Golden Girls.* The obsession with men is still extremely prevalent, manifesting itself in sometimes negative ways with the rest of the staff. Blanche is often accused of skirting her responsibilities around the hotel in order to devote more time to her latest beau. While these were certainly Blanche characteristics in *The Golden Girls,* in the new series her actions affect the entire staff.

The new Blanche is a lot stronger of a character in *The Golden Palace,* although a lot of her perceived strength comes from her bossiness and desire to be in charge. Blanche locks horns with Roland quite a bit due to the fact that he is trying to do his job while Blanche simply wants to be in charge. She normally switches off with Roland in covering front desk duties.

Blanche again ends up with a new love interest in almost every episode. This is another concept which follows from *The Golden Girls.* The men who become Blanche's lovers in *The Golden Palace* are of a more refined group, often appearing to be relatively wealthy.

Blanche has a rather interesting relationship with the new cast members. Roland and Blanche often end up in power struggles as Blanche attempts to control every aspect of the hotel. Chuy and Blanche often make for a great comedic duo as the details of their pasts come out. Finally, Oliver ends up being a sort of adopted grandchild to Blanche. While the youngster also deals with the control issues of Blanche, he is the least affected.

Of the three, Blanche is the carryover character from *The Golden Girls* who is the most changed. Her seemingly obsessive need to be in control and run the hotel her way makes for a very changed Blanche from the southern belle we knew in the first series.

PLEASE BE SEATED...I'D LIKE TO INTRODUCE...
Sophia Spirelli - Petrillo - Weinstock

Sophia Petrillo (her maiden name was never mentioned in the series) was born in Sicily. Her parents also had two other children, Angela and Angelo. According to the many stories she tells, she grew up very poor and was never able to enjoy many pleasures during her youth. At a young age she decided she wanted to leave the poor village she grew up in to relocate to America. Through an arranged marriage in Sicily, Sophia was married briefly to Guido Spirelli - a union that was soon annulled.

Sophia married Salvatore (Sal) Petrillo and the two had three children. Their first born was Dorothy, followed by Phil and finally Gloria. The family remained in Brookyln, New York until all of the children reached adulthood. Sometime in the 1950's (although it was never actually pinpointed when) Sal passed away leaving Sophia alone. Eventually, Sophia would end up in Miami where Dorothy and her husband Stan resided. When Stan and Dorothy divorced, Sophia and Dorothy would become closer, until Sophia suffered a terrible stroke. Dorothy saw fit to place her in a nursing home called Shady Pines.

In the opening episode of *The Golden Girls,* Shady Pines burns down, and therefore Sophia comes to live with the other three girls. The effects of her stroke are still quite evident being that she speaks exactly what is on her mind all the time (a fact that Blanche points out in the pilot episode).

Sophia's stories are often as crazy as Rose's, but she often has a valid point that the girls look for as advice to the numerous problems that they encounter. Most of the stories begin with the year and place that Sophia is speaking of. In some of her stories and lessons, she makes references to the fact that her and her family had mafia connections, although this is never actually said to be true. Many flashbacks that were included in the show depicted Sophia as a younger woman. We also saw her husband Sal in several episodes, however since he was already dead, these were always dreams or flashbacks.

Both of Sophia's siblings appeared on the show, the more prominent being her brother Angelo. Angelo would eventually move to Miami and was featured in a few episodes. Sophia's sister Angela also was said to have moved to Miami, but after one episode, this was never mentioned again in the series.

In later episodes Sophia marries Max Weinstock, an old business partner of her late husband's. While the two feel that they are in love initially, it doesn't take long for them to realize that they were missing their spouses much more than they actually loved each other. The two separated, but agreed to stay married and get together for occasional visits.

Like Rose and Blanche, Sophia would remain and end up on the show *The Golden Palace*.

TIMES AT THE GOLDEN PALACE

Of the three, Sophia is definitely the most closely related character from *The Golden Girls*. The acid tongue and tell-it-like-it-is attitude continues, although, like the others, she now has a full time job operating the hotel. Sophia assumes a role as an assistant chef in the kitchen at the Golden Palace. While there is in initially a disagreement over the kind of food that should be prepared in the kitchen, Chuy and Sophia eventually come to a compromise.

Sophia continues getting into misadventures due to her age and her desire to be an independent woman. As in *The Golden Girls,* she ends up stealing a car, and even takes Oliver with her. But, all in all she does her part to pitch in at the Golden Palace. In spite of her advanced age, she keeps up with the other girls the best she can.

Sophia deals with the "death" of Stan, her ex-son-in-law in one episode. Stan makes a crossover appearance from *The Golden Girls,* stating that he has now gone broke. While she tries to convince the others that the Stan is simply faking his death, none of the others will believe her. As the series closes before the subject is ever covered again, we can assume that Sophia will remain the only character to ever know the real story with Stan.

Sophia's relationship with the other cast members is varied. While she certainly maintains the occasional barrage of insults on everyone, she is also still the same kind old soul from *The Golden Girls.* She has an amazing relationship with Oliver, the youngster of the group.

While it's not possible to remove a character from one show and put her into another without any changes, Sophia seems to accept the change best. Even though she is now helping in a different kitchen, she's basically still the Sophia we know and love.

The Golden Palace

THE EPISODE GUIDE

1- Pilot (The Golden Palace)

Episode Production Number: 01
Filming Location: Hollywood, CA
Original Air Date: September 18, 1992
Episode Length: 22:02
Writer(s): Susan Harris
Director: Terry Hughes

Guest Stars:

Stephen James Carver (Brad)
Tom LaGrua (Thief)
Lee Ryan (I) (Man #1)

Episode Description:

In this, the pilot episode, we see the beginning of *The Golden Palace* as well as the closure of *The Golden Girls.* The writers of the show begin the pilot on the old set of *The Golden Girls,* except that it's pretty obvious the girls are moving out of the house. After a few minutes of dialogue, we learn that they have sold the house in order to get the funds to purchase the Golden Palace, a Miami Beach hotel. Rose shows a bit of concern that things will not work out, but as Blanche explains, it's already too late to change their minds. At the first commercial break, the girls are exited from the house, officially closing *The Golden Girls* forever.

As the show returns, now at the new location, the lobby of the Golden Palace, we see Roland and a young boy named Oliver. We learn that Roland is a worker at the hotel, and Oliver, his foster child. Sophia, Rose and Blanche enter the hotel and announce that they have arrived. Roland has never been informed of who the new owners are and apparently the girls don't exactly look like hotel owners. As such, Roland is a little less than cordial in welcoming them – until Sophia announces that they are the new owners – which causes Roland's demeanor to change significantly. We hear almost immediately that the hotel has its share of problems as Roland brings the new owners up-to-speed about their purchase.

The sparks begin to fly when we learn that the hotel has exactly three employees, and there is a large debt that must be paid by the end of the month in order to allow the girls to keep the hotel. The girls begin to immediately feel that they may have made a huge mistake in purchasing the hotel. But, at this point they have no choice but to try and find a way to raise the money to pay the loan. To make matters worse, Sophia and the current cook Chuy have a fight about the type of food that should be cooked in the hotel kitchen, causing Chuy to quit.

In the end, a group of travel agents shows up to put the Golden Palace to the test. Even though they have a few rough moments, they are able to convince the travel agents that their hotel is of first class style. Chuy the cook will eventually return as well, and is able to reach a compromise with Sophia.

2 - Promotional Considerations

Episode Production Number: 02
Filming Location: Hollywood, CA
Original Air Date: September 25, 1992
Episode Length: 21:33
Writer(s): Jim Vallely
Director: Lex Passaris

Guest Stars:

Bobcat Goldthwait (Gordon McCray Cosay)
Gibby Brand (Mr. Ken McGowan)

Episode Description:

In the second installment of *The Golden Palace,* we see the group discussing the need to bring in more customers to the hotel. They all seem to agree that advertising is the right way, but can't decide how. Sophia suggests handing out fliers for free margaritas, but no one else agrees. Rose seems to have her own ideas, but no one seems interested in listening to her.

In the mean time, a prestigious writer is going to be a guest of the hotel. Blanche and Roland argue about who should be the one to check him in. Eventually, Blanche indicates that she is the owner of the hotel and should be the one to check in the writer. Roland, although unhappy, allows Blanche to get her way. During the episode, Blanche has run-ins with other employees, essentially insisting that everyone run everything past her before decisions are made. While everyone is obviously annoyed, it is Roland who really is bothered by Blanche's attitude.

Soon, Rose will announce that she has found a way to get more money for the hotel – she has worked out a deal with *The Barbara LaGrange Show.* The show will provide free advertising for the hotel, and in exchange, the hotel will provide accommodations for guests of the show. All seems great until a promo airs for the show stating that the guests for the following day will be men who kill and have been set free. Immediately following the shock of watching the promo, a very odd man walks in. The entire hotel staff is convinced he is a killer.

Later that evening, Blanche and Roland begin a dialogue which Roland sees as Blanche apologizing to him because the hotel is now falling apart. The supposed killer, Gordon, comes out of his room and gives a few words of advice about how everyone needs to feel needed in this world. This advice allows Roland and Blanche to put away their ill feelings towards each other.

At the end of the episode, Sophia has decided to quit her flier campaign due to a severe hangover. We also see that while they are watching the *Barbara LaGrange Show,* they make a very important discovery – Gordon was actually a therapist at a local prison.

3 - Miles, We Hardly Knew Ye

Episode Production Number: 06 **Filming Location: Hollywood, CA** **Original Air Date: October 2, 1992** **Episode Length: 21:29** **Writer(s): Marc Cherry, Jamie Wooten** **Director: Peter D. Beyt**	**Guest Stars:** Harold Gould (Miles Webber) Marty Brinton (Man #1) Mary Pat Gleason (Woman) Robert Beecher (Older Man)

Episode Description:

In this episode, we see the first cross-over from *The Golden Girls* as Miles enters the picture. Rose takes a call from Miles, after which she tells Blanche that Miles has yet again cancelled their plans for the evening. Blanche feels for Rose, and indicates that maybe it is time for their relationship to receive some spicing up.

A few moments later, Roland and Blanche are going through old guest log books and continually find the name Miles Weber. Blanche immediately begins to assume that Miles has been cheating on Rose for several years. Rose becomes convinced that Blanche's assumption is true. Rose waits for Miles to appear before she brings up the problem.

Oliver takes to using a lost and found box to make extra money. Until, that is, Sophia explains that he is extorting the guests. Of course, Sophia extorts Oliver for five dollars to keep her mouth shut.

When Miles does finally show, Rose confronts him. Miles adamantly denies the accusation from Rose and storms out. Rose leaves the room as Roland comes in. He informs Blanche that the hotel guest known as Miles Weber is not Rose's Miles. Now, Blanche must tell Rose that she was wrong. However, she refuses to admit her error for several hours. It's not until Roland tells Rose the truth that she actually knows Blanche's accusation was completely off. When Rose finally does confront Blanche, the sparks really fly and the two have a horrible fight. Rose swears off her friendship with Blanche.

Rose and Miles being to reconcile everything. During the conversation, Miles admits that there *is* someone else, a woman named Fern. Miles admits that Blanche really wasn't that far off in her accusation because *he was* seeing two women at the same time. Rose asks Miles to leave. This effectively begins to remove the character of Miles from the story line.

Blanche apologizes for not telling Rose in a more timely manner. Rose breaks down and Blanche provides her comfort.

4 - One Old Lady To Go

Episode Production Number: 05
Filming Location: Hollywood, CA
Original Air Date: October 9, 1992
Episode Length: 23:09
Writer(s): Jim Vallely
Director: Lex Passaris

Guest Stars:

Margaret Cho (Dr. Fong)
Kelly Cinnante (Officer #2)
Michael Francis Clarke (Officer #1)
Annie O'Donnell (Charlene)
Anne Haney (Vivian)

Episode Description:

As this episode opens, Sophia enters the kitchen and states that business in the dining room has been very slow. She indicates that she needs extra money to pay for new teeth.

When Oliver comes home, the others are able to determine that he has a new girlfriend at school. This worries both Chuy and Roland as they know that they'll have to have a talk with him about sex.

Rose has been feeding an older woman named Vivian for some time. Even though it seems like a very harmless situation at the beginning, we get to see that Vivian has her own set of issues. She apparently has a very advanced case of Alzheimer's and is now convinced that Rose is her daughter. Rose insists that Vivian be allowed to stay in the hotel. The others concede.

The hotel has been receiving a steady stream of calls which are meant for a Chinese food restaurant also called the Golden Palace. When Roland tells Sophia that they have been receiving over twenty calls a day, Sophia has an idea to make more money – she begins a Chinese take-out business run out of the Golden Palace kitchen.

Blanche and Roland finally convince Rose to turn Vivian over the authorities. At the same time, they officially shut down Sophia's Chinese food business. But, when the police show up and are informed that the old lady they are supposed to be picking up is in the back room, and it's Sophia who ends up being taken away.

The sex talk Roland and Chuy were to give ends up being very short-lived. Even though Chuy attempts to lend a hand, Roland takes over and handles the conversation himself. Oliver indicates he only likes the girl in question as a friend anyway.

When Sophia is returned by the police, Vivian's daughter accompanies them. It turns out that she had gone to the police at the same time Sophia was brought in. Mother and daughter are reunited and Rose can now be at peace with the Vivian situation.

5 - Ebbtide for The Defense

Episode Production Number: 08
Filming Location: Hollywood, CA
Original Air Date: October 16, 1992
Episode Length: 22:55
Writer(s): Marc Sotkin
Director: Peter D. Beyt

Guest Stars:

Christopher Collins (Angel)
Steve Hytner (Burrows)
Gregory Sierra (Rubin)
Robert Beecher (Older Man)

Episode Description:

As this episode opens, Roland has volunteered to help out in the kitchen. It becomes obvious that he may not be much of a help at all with his fear of touching dead poultry.

The hotel has taken on lawyers as guests who are attending a local conference. Ever since they have arrived, they have been threatening to sue for every little problem. Blanche and Rose are especially looking forward to them leaving. During a discussion, we learn that Rose double booked the rooms after looking at a St. Olaf calendar upside down. They believe a group of judges will be arriving before the attorneys check out.

Soon, a new chef named Rubin is hired to help Chuy in the kitchen. As soon as Chuy sees Rubin he bursts into a fit of anger. It turns out that Rubin, Chuy's friend, had been having an affair with Chuy's wife – which led to Chuy's divorce. Despite Chuy's complaints, the hotel needs an extra person in the kitchen, and as such, Chuy concedes to allowing Rubin to stay.

Now, another problem surfaces as we learn that the hotel has just lost their liability insurance. Roland explains that with no liability insurance, one accident could lead to a lawsuit - not a situation they want to have with a hotel full of lawyers.

Rose convinces an attorney to share a room with one of the judges. But, just then we discover that the "judges" are actually a motorcycle gang. The attorney informs Blanche that if anything happens to him he will sue.

Oddly enough, the motorcycle gang member and the attorney actually get along really well. The gang member even gives the attorney a tattoo. Thankfully, there is no longer a threat of a lawsuit.

In the end, Chuy finds the strength inside himself to forgive his friend Rubin for destroying his marriage. Even though hurt feelings are still present, Rubin is leaving the Golden Palace, so Chuy decides to bring some closure to the situation.

6 - Can't Stand Losing You

<table>
<tr><td>

Episode Production Number: 07
Filming Location: Hollywood, CA
Original Air Date: October 23, 1992
Episode Length: 24:01
Writer(s): Mitchell Hurwitz
Director: Peter D. Beyt

</td><td>

Guest Stars:

Kim Fields (Trisha)
Sonya Hunt (Roy)
Monte Landis (Mr. Ricchuitti)
Monica Allison (Joanne)

</td></tr>
</table>

Episode Description:

Rose and Blanche have decided that Roland is a workaholic and needs a little excitement in his life. They believe that a woman may be the answer and begin to argue about who would be the better matchmaker. While Rose maintains that her loving history with men makes for a much better understanding of a great relationship, Blanche insists that the sheer volume of men she has had makes her the clear winner.

The hotel is then presented with a golden opportunity when the talk show *Wake Up Miami* contacts them and requests that Chuy appear on their show. Even though Sophia insists she is a better cook, Chuy states that his history of television experience (which is minor to say the least) should make him the clear choice to appear on the show.

Rose states that she will soon win the contest her and Blanche are having as they attempt to find a woman for Roland. Blanche immediately needs to find a woman to present to Roland – and she finds that woman in the form of a meat delivery person. This idea fails horribly.

Soon, the date that Rose found, Joanne, appears and Roland is more than impressed. When the two leave on a date, Blanche is crushed fearing that Rose is a better match-maker than her. Just then Oliver states that he believes Roland never got over his ex Tricia. Of course, Blanche takes it upon herself to contact the ex and soon enough Tricia is on her way to Miami.

Once Roland finds out that Blanche brought Tricia back into his life, he is upset. He doesn't understand why Blanche just can't stay out of his life. But, even though he does not want anything to do with Tricia, he can't seem to be honest with her.

Roland finally decides that he needs to have it out with Tricia once and for all. He tells her exactly how he feels and she seems to understand. She also lets Roland know that she will be receiving a very large inheritance soon.

In the end, Rose celebrates the fact that her matchmaking abilities exceed that of Blanche.

7 - Seems Like Old Times (1)

Episode Production Number: 09
Filming Location: Hollywood, CA
Original Air Date: October 30, 1992
Episode Length: 23:02
Writer(s): Jamie Wooten, Marc Cherry
Director: Lex Passaris

Guest Stars:

Bertila Damas (Beverly)
Bea Arthur (Dorothy Zbornak
Hollingsworth)
Kent Zbornak (Cab Driver)
Henry Polic II (Man #1)

Episode Description:

Ah, finally the four ladies are reunited again! This episode features primary member of *The Golden Girls* cast, Bea Arthur. This installment was heavily promoted due to the appearance of Bea, and would be one of the highest rated episodes of *The Golden Palace.*

As the episode opens, we see the girls excited and feverishly preparing for Dorothy's arrival. It has been over four months since she has seen the girls and has never been to the hotel before. The girls anticipate plenty of good times and cheesecake as they regroup with each other.

While he does go to court and is now officially divorced, Chuy is feeling pangs of loneliness as he realizes the finality of the divorce. Roland attempts to lend a hand and tells Chuy that to get his confidence back, he should hit on the first woman he sees. Of course, the first woman to walk in is Dorothy. After being shot down by Dorothy, Roland decides Chuy needs a guy's night out and brings him to a strip club.

The following morning, Chuy is no where to be found so the girls ask Dorothy to help out. She agrees, but is bothered by the amount of work she witnesses Sophia performing. Sophia doesn't share the same concern as Dorothy, stating that she works this hard all the time.

When Chuy finally surfaces, he divulges that he got drunk the night before and is now re-married. While the rest of the staff is shocked, Chuy states that he needs some time to think about his new bride and what he has done.

Meanwhile, Dorothy calls her husband Lucas and states that she wants Sophia to come and live with them. Lucas is okay with the decision and this leads Dorothy to having an important talk with the three girls. They all resent what Dorothy is planning to do, but Dorothy states that this is the best thing for her mother.

In the end, Sophia has gone missing with nothing but a note left behind.

8 - Seems Like Old Times (2)

Episode Production Number: 10
Filming Location: Hollywood, CA
Original Air Date: November 6, 1992
Episode Length: 22:57
Writer(s): Jim Vallely
Director: Lex Passaris

Guest Stars:

Furley Lumpkin (Security Guard)
Jack Black (Cab Driver)
Miguel Sandoval (Ramone)
Carol Leifer (Meredith)
Bertila Damas (Beverly)
Bea Arthur (Dorothy Zbornak Hollingsworth)
Mark Kubr (Brick)

Episode Description:

Continuing from the last episode, the girls are in shock when they have now learned that Sophia has taken to hiding out at Shady Pines. The shock of her leaving, coupled with the fact that she has taken refuge in a place she had always expressed a hatred for is too much for Dorothy. The bickering between the girls about where Sophia should live continues until the girls eventually take off to find Sophia at Shady Pines.

Meanwhile, Chuy continues to have problems with his new bride Beverly. It seems that she won't sleep with Chuy to consummate the marriage. Even though he confides in Roland, he isn't receiving the answers he wants from anyone. But, things get much worse when Chuy suddenly receives a surprise visit from Ramone, Beverly's ex boyfriend. Ramone tells Chuy that if he ever hurts Beverly there will be severe consequences.

When the girls arrive at Shady Pines, it is quite different than they imagined. Instead of finding a retirement home where nothing works and everyone is miserable, the girls find everyone in the lap of luxury. Sophia has just completed getting a massage. Although, she again tries to convince the girls to leave her in the "terrible" conditions, Dorothy refuses and Sophia is brought back to the Golden Palace.

Chuy finally decides to talk to Beverly about their situation. He explains to her that he simply doesn't love her. When Chuy mentions Ramone, Beverly's attitude changes immediately as she is able to see that Ramone loved her. In fact, the only reason she married Chuy was to make Ramone jealous. When Chuy mentions divorce, Beverly states there is no need as they were never married in the first place.

Finally, Dorothy is able to see that the girls need Sophia at the Golden Palace. It's also clear that Dorothy now has a new life established in Atlanta with Lucas. As the episode closes, all of the girls go back to their responsibilities at the hotel. Dorothy is a little heartbroken and she misses the girls. But, without a word, she picks up her bags and exits.

9 - Just A Gigolo

Episode Production Number: 11
Filming Location: Hollywood, CA
Original Air Date: November 13, 1992
Episode Length: 22:04
Writer(s): Tony Delia
Director: Lex Passaris

Guest Stars:

Barry Bostwick (Nick DeCarlo)
Phil Proctor (Vincent Vale)

Episode Description:

As the episode opens, Roland is excited as there will be a motivational speaker holding a conference at the hotel. The name of the seminar "Ready, Willing and Able," seems to confuse Chuy and Blanche as to the content.

Soon, we are introduced to a Nick Decarlo, a guest staying at the hotel. All of the girls, including Sophia, are head-over-heels in love with him. Nick indicates that he has a problem – a check he was expecting will be late and he needs to work in the kitchen in order to work off his debt from staying in the hotel. He also indicates, to the shock of everyone, that he is a gigolo looking for his next target. Even though none of the girls agree with his lifestyle, none of them seem too bothered to have him around the hotel as a temporary employee.

Later that day, Blanche is disappointed to hear that her date for the evening will no longer be able to attend the function they had planned on – because he died. Even though Rose doesn't like the idea, Blanche accepts a proposal from Nick to accompany her.

Meanwhile, at the seminar, Roland and Chuy listen to the beginning of the presentation and learn that all participants of the seminar must eventually walk across hot coals. Chuy states that this is fear of his and there is no way he'll be able to do it.

Later that evening Nick and Blanche return. The passion between them is too great and they end up sharing a kiss. The next day, the rest of the staff indicates that their relationship is not the best idea, but it's pretty obvious that Blanche will do what she wants to do.

At the hot coals walking portion of the seminar, Chuy conquers his fear and is able to walk across the coals. As soon as he does, he also convinces Roland to do the same.

Rose discovers that Nick is not a gigolo at all, but actually a conman. She confronts Nick and explains that she will turn him in if he does not leave the Golden Palace immediately. This occurs just in time as Blanche was about to give Nick a check for $1500.00.

10 - Marriage On The Rocks, With A Twist

Episode Production Number: 12
Filming Location: Hollywood, CA
Original Air Date: November 20, 1992
Episode Length: 21:19
Writer(s): Marc Cherry, Jamie Wooten
Director: Peter D. Beyt

Guest Stars:

Bruce A. Young (George Wilson)
Harvey Korman (Bill)
Tim Conway (Milton)
Ja'net DuBois (Louise Wilson)
Edward Penn (Man #1)

Episode Description:

Blanche is excited as radio show hosts Bill and Milton will be broadcasting a live show from the hotel. Bill and Milton have a long history of playing practical jokes on people.

Roland receives a call from his parents and is immediately concerned that, because his father called him a boyhood nickname, his dog Taffy died. However, when his parents finally do show up they indicate that they will be getting a divorce. Roland is shocked to hear the news and also discovers that, in fact, Taffy *is* dead.

At the live broadcast, Bill and Milton have a great time poking fun at Blanche indicating that she is either a transvestite or a transsexual. Blanche is able to keep her sense of humor for a little while but eventually gets sick of their treatment. Then, the attention turns to an apparent trivia contest where Rose is targeted as a contestant. In actuality, this is the beginning of their latest practical joke. Bill indicates that the other host Milton must stay in a tank submerged in water until Rose answers 3 questions. She answers the first two fine, but is then presented with a question with an extremely extensive answer as the third. In the mean time, Milton "drowns" in the water. Rose is devastated.

Roland agrees to allow Blanche to try and help his parents work out their issues. During the conversation, Roland's parents share their grievances with each other, but Blanche can do nothing but talk about herself. Roland eventually asks Blanche to leave and indicates that if his parents are going to divorce, he will have to accept it.

Chuy forces Sophia to tell Rose the truth about the fact that Milton is not dead. During the process, a "ghost" of Milton shows up and scares Rose who runs into the kitchen. We hear gun-shots and soon Rose emerges from the kitchen with a gun stating she has sent the ghost back to where he came from. Sophia is mortified. But, it turns out that it was really a practical joke to be played on Sophia instead. Rose was a part of the plan the whole time.

11 - Camp Town Races Aren't Nearly As Much Fun As They Used To Be

Episode Production Number: 04
Filming Location: Hollywood, CA
Original Air Date: December 14, 1992
Episode Length: 24:09
Writer(s): Marc Sotkin
Director: Lex Passaris

Guest Stars:

Charles Napier (Mr. Smith #1)
Arthur Eckdahl (Mr. Smith #2)
Camille Ameen (Mrs. Smith #1)
Joyce Meadows (Mrs. Pinkerman)
Joe Alaskey (Mr. Smith #3)

Episode Description:

Blanche has scheduled an organization known as the Daughters of the Traditional South to stay at the hotel.

At the front desk, Rose is having an issue with the fact that a couple is checking in under the name "Mr. and Mrs. Smith." Rose is well aware of whom the fictitious Mr. Smith really is, and she knows that he is married to a different woman. Just then, Roland notices the announcement sign for the Daughters of the Traditional South. He states that he is uncomfortable with the organization being guests at the hotel due to the racial attitudes such an organization possesses. Again, Blanche dismisses the accusations as being blown out of proportion and states that they need the business. But, when Blanche hangs a Confederate flag, Roland gets really upset and decides to quit as soon as he finds other employment.

During a break, Rose tells a St. Olaf story about how she once unintentionally cheated on Charlie. It turns out that her and Charlie were dressed up as characters in preparation for a crazy lovemaking session. With the lights off, Rose inadvertently got into bed with the wrong man. This is how she explains her concern with people using the hotel for adulteries.

Soon, Rose breaks into the room of "Mr. and Mrs. Smith" and completely disturbs them. As they are checking out, Blanche gets angry with Rose for forcing a good customer out.

When Roland enters the lobby and the prejudice of one of the organization members becomes apparent, Blanche sees her wrongdoing. Where she was constantly masking it with traditional values, Roland points out that some of these values are rooted in prejudice.

Blanche and Roland agree to try and understand each others values and feelings in the future. As such, Roland decides to stay on at the Golden Palace.

12 - It's Beginning To Look A Lot (Less) Like Christmas

<table>
<tr><td>

Episode Production Number: 14
Filming Location: Hollywood, CA
Original Air Date: December 18, 1992
Episode Length: 22:09
Writer(s): Jonathan Schmock
Director: Peter D. Beyt

</td><td>

Guest Stars:

Susan Norfleet (Wanda)
Nick Toth (Dr. Norman Charles)
Isaac Ocampo (Young Chuy)

</td></tr>
</table>

Episode Description:

It's Christmas time at the Golden Palace and everyone is looking forward to the festivities – except Chuy. He explains that Christmas has always been a rotten time for him.

Soon, Roland gets a call and volunteers to play Santa for a local children's home. At this point, Rose explains that Roland must be completely prepared to play Santa for the children. Using Sophia as a "child," and with Rose's instruction, Roland practices the nuances of being a Santa Claus.

To everyone's disappointment the leader of a support group shows up with a request. He states that the Christmas decorations in the lobby have to go because his patients are very fragile and will not respond well to the decorations. Even though everyone is disappointed, the hotel needs the business, so the decorations come down. Chuy is more than thrilled, announcing again that he dislikes Christmas.

That night, Chuy is visited by three ghosts – first by Rose, the ghost of Christmas past. She brings Chuy to a time 30 years in the past and shows him how his father had an impact on the people in his neighborhood by giving them a place to eat in his restaurant. Next , Blanche shows up and shows Chuy a scene which involves the girls and Roland celebrating Christmas in a freezer. During the dialogue, Blanche states that they cannot open presents until Chuy joins them - hence Blacnhe's role - "The Ghost of Chiristmas Presents." Finally, Sophia shows up as the ghost of Christmas yet to come. She shows Chuy a scene where all of the girls and Roland are workers for the hotel. Chuy has puchased the hotel after swindling Blanche out of it, and they are all now working in slave-like conditions.

Once Chuy finally wakes up, he has a changed attitude about the Christmas holiday. He interrupts the support group meeting, but ends up telling the story of his dream and convinces the group to join in on the holiday festivites.

13 - Rose And Fern

Episode Production Number: 13
Filming Location: Hollywood, CA
Original Air Date: January 8, 1993
Episode Length: 22:01
Writer(s): Marc Sotkin
Director: Peter D. Beyt

Guest Stars:

Hartley Silver (Man #1)
Harold Gould (Miles Webber)
Nanette Fabray (Fern)

Episode Description:

As the episode opens, Chuy and Sophia have a quick dialogue about how the oven needs to be repaired. Unfortunately, every time the oven repair man shows up, he apparently sleeps with Blanche and never fixes the oven.

At the front desk, Rose has been continually receiving calls from Miles convincing her that he wants to get back together. Blanche indicates that maybe she should explore the possibility, seeing as how she still has feelings for him. Rose is unsure of how to feel about the situation.

Roland finds that someone has been stealing from the till and mentions the issue to Blanche. The two of them decide to launch their own investigation to try and find out who the thief is. They are both dismayed that someone they work with and trust is stealing from them.

The girls have been contracted to hold a wedding. Blanche and Rose work on the details of the wedding, both of them ecstatic as the hotel really needs the business. Rose meets with Fern, the bride to be, and discusses the details of the wedding. Blanche talks up the hotel, but when Miles enters and indicates that Fern is his fiancé, Rose is struck down with grief. As Miles and Fern leave, Rose is both depressed and feels foolish as she thought Miles was attempting to reconcile.

Eventually, Roland catches Blanche removing cash from a cash box. When he confronts her about it, Blanche states that she was using the money for "business purposes." Roland explains to her that taking money with actually leaving a receipt is technically embezzling. Blanche has no idea that what she is doing is wrong – she assures Roland things will be different in the future.

As the episode closes, Rose and Blanche watch Miles get married. While it's obviously a very difficult thing for Rose to do, it is the closure she needs to finally let the Miles situation come to a close. This effectively removes Miles from the story line.

14 - Runaways

Episode Production Number: 03
Filming Location: Hollywood, CA
Original Air Date: January 15, 1993
Episode Length: 22:59
Writer(s): Mitchell Hurwitz
Director: Lex Passaris

Guest Stars:

David Jay Willis (Mr. Wormer)
Alexander Folk (The Cop)
Charles Bouvier (Mr. Fisk)
Joely Fisher (Paula Webb)
Hansford Rowe (Mr. Seigel)
Michael Fairman (Ernie Niles)

Episode Description:

As the episode opens, Chuy and Sophia share a quick banter about who is in charge in the kitchen. Sophia then tries to get both Chuy, and later Blanche, to lend out their cars so she can go downtown for some errands – they both refuse.

The Golden Palace is holding a big sweet sixteen party for their banker's daughter. Even though the rest of the staff is ready to pitch in, Blanche seems more concerned with personalized pens she ordered for the hotel and the fact that she a date with a new beau, Ernie Niles.

The staff is holding auditions for party entertainment. At exactly the same moment, the phone rings with a call from the Department of Family Services. It turns out that Oliver's mother is out of rehab and is ready to come for him.

Blanche comes in and announces that she is in love. She doesn't seem to care that her work is slipping at the hotel and even though the others express their concern, she is more concerned with Ernie. Even when the pens she ordered show up with a severe typo, she completely skirts her work responsibility. The other staff members indicate their displeasure again.

In the mean time, Sophia has now stolen the car of a man staying at the hotel. She has taken Oliver with her and is now on the open road. Amusingly enough, the scene opens with the car's left blinker continually on – just as Chuy predicts at the beginning of the episode.

Oliver's mother shows up, but of course Oliver is not there. Chuy and Roland are able to convince Oliver's mother, Paula, to come back later. The police bring Sophia and Oliver in a few minutes later and leave the two in the custody of Roland and Rose.

Later, Blanche returns and explains that her relationship is over. After a talk, the others on staff decide to forgive her. Roland comes in and although he is upset about the loss of Oliver, he is glad to see Blanche again being responsible. Oliver is now removed from the show.

15 - Heartbreak Hotel

Episode Production Number: 16
Filming Location: Hollywood, CA
Original Air Date: January 29, 1993
Episode Length: 26:01
Writer(s): Julie Thacker
Director: Lex Passaris

Guest Stars:

Dick Van Patten (Taylor)
Pamela Dunlap (Dr. Ursula)

Episode Description:

The Golden Palace has a romantic weekend getaway planned. While Roland feels that the flow of guest reservations is due to all the perks the hotel is offering, Rose states that the visiting "Love Doctor" is more the reason. When Sophia hears of the presentation by the Love Doctor, she decides she wants to go to help with her apparent sexual problems.

Blanche appears and states that an old friend of hers named Taylor, who she was extremely interested in, is coming to stay at the hotel. Blanche explains that she and her college roommate Lauren were in competition over Taylor years ago. Blanche eventually lost the competition.

A few hours later, Taylor arrives and is immediately attracted to Rose, who is alone at the front desk. Rose reciprocates the feelings of attractiveness and soon the two are flirting with each other – just as Blanche walks in. It doesn't take but a few seconds for Blanche to discover that there is attractiveness between the two – something she does not take to very well.

Taylor and Rose go on one date, and then plan for another the following night. This is too much for Blanche to take. Just as Taylor and Rose are about to leave for their second date, Roland begins receiving complains that none of Rose's responsibilities at the hotel have been completed. She adamantly states that she has completed all of her work and in fact, several hours before. Roland asks her to go and check on the problems – she does, and leaves Taylor in the lobby. Soon enough, Blanche shows up and states that, as Rose cannot go, she will go out with Taylor. Even though Taylor is confused, he does leave with Blanche.

After another fight ensues, Taylor comes up with a suggestion that the three of them have dinner together the following evening. Both Rose and Blanche agree to Taylor's idea. However, both are still convinced they will win Taylor's hand after the dinner.

The following night, a big fight ensues at the dinner with Taylor. Blanche storms out and Rose goes after her. Rose asks Blanche of her friendship is more important than a man. Blanche states that it is. As a test, Blanche successfully sits in the kitchen and allows Rose to continue her date with Taylor uninterrupted.

16 - Señor Stinky Learns Absolutely Nothing About Life

Episode Production Number: 19
Filming Location: Hollywood, CA
Original Air Date: February 5, 1993
Episode Length: 22:53
Writer(s): Marc Sotkin
Director: Peter D. Beyt

Guest Stars:

Stephen James Carver (Brad)
Ricardo Montalban (Lawrence Gentry)

Episode Description:

As the episode opens, Blanche opens a notification stating that the Golden Palace is being sued by The Mecca Hotel. The owner, Mr. Gentry, claims that the Golden Palace parking lot is on his property. As usual, Blanche indicates that she can use her sexuality to solve the issue.

Soon, Roland enters with a volleyball team sponsored by the hotel. Blanche immediately takes to flirting with and chasing a member of the team, the pool guy Brad. Chuy expresses his disappointment that he is not on the team, however he is simply fed excuses. However, when Rose demonstrates some skills, she is suddenly on the team.

Blanche arrives home from a business appointment where she flirted with a bank manager trying to get more credit. The manager became upset and threw her out. The others explain that she needs to stop using sex to get what she wants.

During a business meeting with the neighboring hotel owner, Mr. Gentry, Blanche finds herself very attracted to him. Although he is attracted to her as well, and finds it extremely difficult, she is able to resist her attraction. When he asks why she is denying her feelings, Blanche states that she is trying to complete a business transaction and personal feelings cannot come into play. They do agree do come up with an amicable solution to the parking lot issue.

At the final volleyball game, Roland and Brad are about to win when Brad suddenly hurts his ankle. Rose is cheer leading, so Chuy comes in. But, when Chuy misses a ball in his direction, they lose the game. Roland completely loses his cool and completely humiliates Chuy. However, later Roland realizes how much he hurt Chuy and apologizes for his actions.

Blanche and Mr. Gentry eventually do date, but only after business is done. They agree to keep their business and personal lives completely separate from each other.

17 - Say Goodbye, Rose

Episode Production Number: 20
Filming Location: Hollywood, CA
Original Air Date: February 12, 1993
Episode Length: 22:01
Writer(s): Jim Vallely
Director: Peter D. Beyt

Guest Stars:

Eddie Albert (Bill Douglas)
George Burns (Himself)
Bill Engvall (Matthew Devereaux)

Episode Description:

The Golden Palace is holding a comedy competition which has the whole staff busy setting up and interviewing talent. Even though Roland doesn't like the idea, Chuy insists on being part of the show as well, with an act he calls "Corny Castillos."

At the front desk, Blanche explains that her son Matthew is coming to the hotel to visit. At the same time, a man named Bill Douglas enters the hotel to check in. As Rose enters the lobby, she sees Bill and immediately screams. She runs into the kitchen where she explains that Bill looks almost exactly like her late husband Charlie.

When Matthew arrives, he announces that he has something to tell Blanche. Blanche has herself convinced that Matthew is gay. In fact, he has come to tell Blanche that he is giving up a stock broker job to become a comedian. He also wants to be in the comedy show. Blanche does not understand his decision and does not accept it. She is also upset that he has chosen to make personal jokes about her.

Rose and Bill go out on a date and eventually share a kiss at the end of the evening. When she shares this update with the other staff later, they express their disapproval.

Blanche indicates that she will not be going to the comedy show if Matthew is going to perform. The girls listen to a story about how George used to do some crazy, embarrassing things when they were first married. Eventually Blanche sees that she should allow Matthew to be himself and follow his dreams.

Rose and Bill talk and she admits how she really feels and that her feelings for Bill were closely tied to how much she misses Charlie. Bill allows Rose to say goodbye to Charlie through him. After she says her goodbyes, Bill exits. Sophia shows up to a devastated Rose and brings her in to meet a special guest – George Burns. After a short attempt to cheer Rose up through comedy, George takes the stage at the comedy show and does a quick routine.

18 - You've Lost That Living Feeling

Episode Production Number: 18
Filming Location: Hollywood, CA
Original Air Date: February 19, 1993
Episode Length: 24:07
Writer(s): Marco Pennette
Director: Peter D. Beyt

Guest Stars:

Eric Christmas (Mr. Gerald Davenport)
Bill Morey (Mr. Mitchelson)
Stephen Root (Mr. Tucker)
Jeanne Mori (Marion Kim)

Episode Description:

The staff is throwing a grand reopening celebration at the Golden Palace. In an attempt to add to the celebration and bring in more guests, Rose has arranged for restaurant critic Gerald Davenport to visit. While everyone sees this as a great opportunity, they are not aware that Chuy has a past with this man – and it's not good. Davenport once gave Chuy a very bad review. Now, Chuy is filled with angst, worried that Davenport will give him another poor review.

The girls continue to prepare the re-opening celebration and soon the critic arrives. Chuy and Davenport have a bad relationship almost immediately – it's obvious that they both remember each other from past dealings. While Chuy does his best to create his best dish, nothing can prepare Chuy for what he finds when he enters the dining room. As Chuy attempts to check on the critic, he discovers that Davenport is dead. Now Chuy is paranoid as he believes that he accidentally put poison in the man's food. The girls initially refuse this idea, but realizing that Chuy has a bad past with him makes the possibility all the more real.

The girls decide to help Chuy by hiding the body of the dead critic – a task which becomes increasingly more difficult. First, Blanche is running a television interview crew around the hotel attempting to give them a good story, hoping to drum up more business. Then, a surprise visit from a health inspector makes things really crazy. Of course, Blanche jumps on the inspector attempting to remove the possibility of him discovering the dead body.

Craziness ensues as the entire staff ends up having to move the body from place to place in order to keep outsiders from finding out what is going on. At one point, Rose ends up in bed with Mr. Michelson, a travel agent whom the staff was hoping to impress. Eventually the staff is caught with the body. But, they are able to convince everyone that Davenport is drunk, not dead.

In the end, we learn that Mr. Davenport actually died of a massive coronary and not from Chuy's mishap. All is well as the hotel has also passed its health inspection and is going to be recommended as a great place to stay by the travel agent.

19 - A New Leash On Life

Episode Production Number: 15
Filming Location: Hollywood, CA
Original Air Date: April 2, 1993
Episode Length: 24:02
Writer(s): Marco Pennette
Director: Lex Passaris

Guest Stars:

Ken Kercheval (Charlie Sardisco)
Ja'net DuBois (Louise Wilson)
Daryl Roach (Man #1)

Episode Description:

As the episode opens, Sophia hears news that her friend Gladys has broken her hip and there-fore cannot take a planned trip to Los Angeles to see a taping of *The Price is Right.* However Sophia must first find the money to purchase the plane tickets.

Roland's mom Louise has been visiting, just following her divorce. But, problems occur when he lands a date with a woman he has been pursuing for a while and cannot spend the evening with her. Louise understands and tells Roland to keep his date.

Soon a man who is racing Greyhounds at the local track shows up. Blanche shows an instant attraction and Sophia sees this as a way to get money to pay for her trip to Los Angeles. The trainer, Ken, invites the two of them to join him at the track.

When Roland returns, he learns that his mom and Chuy have been out all day together. This concerns Roland as he does not want his mom to be dating anyone, much less Chuy. When Roland witnesses Chuy giving Louise a peck on the lips, he really loses his cool, causing an argument between him and Chuy.

When they are leaving for the race, Ken explains to Rose that if his dog loses the race, the dog will be put down. Rose, completely distraught over the idea, ends up going to the track and actually steals the dog. She then paints spots on the dog to camouflage her. The trainer returns and takes possession of the dog for an upcoming race. Rose is again extremely upset.

Soon, Chuy and Louise return to the Golden Palace. When they indicate that they went to a hotel together, Roland loses all control. But, it turns out that Chuy and Louise are just friends and are going to a divorce support group together.

When the trainer returns, he tells Rose that the dog came in fifth. At Rose's insistence, he de-cides to give the dog to her. Rose decides that she will find an adoption agency for Greyhounds and give the dog up to save its life.

20 - Pro And Concierge

Episode Production Number: 22
Filming Location: Hollywood, CA
Original Air Date: April 9, 1993
Episode Length: 23:48
Writer(s): Kevin Rooney
Director: Lex Passaris

Guest Stars:

Robert Rockwell (Mr. Cochran)
Georgie Cranford (The Kid)

Episode Description:

Rose and Blanche both agree that they should be sending Sophia on a vacation. She has not been getting much done at the hotel and the upcoming guest list is slim. So, they both figure that it's a great time to get her some well deserved rest.

Roland enters and talks to Chuy about the fact that he has been offered a job at the prestigious Carlton Hotel. Even though Roland will not be taking the job, he makes Chuy swear to keep quiet. Later, when Chuy is in the lobby, he lets the news slip to the girls. Scared they are going to lose him, the girls try to come up with ideas on how to raise money to give Roland a raise.

Sophia decides to take her vacation, except that she decides to take it in the Golden Palace. Even though the girls initially don't agree, they eventually give in and allow Sophia to take the penthouse suite.

When Roland begins to talk to Blanche about the Carlton Hotel, Blanche proceeds to fire him. Roland tries to talk to Blanche, but cannot convince her to change her mind. Soon, the girls begin interviewing to find a replacement. Chuy eventually interviews for the position as well, but of course is turned down. The girls also ask Sophia to come back from her "vacation" to help out, but she refuses.

Later, Rose confronts Blanche causing her to finally admit that she fired Roland to allow him to get the job at the Carlton. Unfortunately, the Carlton has heard he was fired and decides not to hire him. He has taken a job at a bicycle rental shop.

Chuy, who can never keep his mouth shut, eventually tells the girls where Roland is. After they go down to the, shop and beg him, Roland accepts their offer to come back.

In the end, Roland does get his raise as Blanche has figured out how to cut a few corners.

21 - Tad

Episode Production Number: 24 **Filming Location: Hollywood, CA** **Original Air Date: April 16, 1993** **Episode Length: 22:43** **Writer(s): Marc Cherry, Jamie Wooten** **Director: Peter D. Beyt**	**Guest Stars:** Ned Beatty (Tad Hollingsworth) Patrick Culliton (The Taxi Driver)

Episode Description:

As the episode opens, Sophia has been making her special Sicilian pizza and is feeding the staff. Blanche comes in and is questioned by everyone about her trip to Chattanooga. Apparently, she has been going to the same destination for years, but always refuses to elaborate on what she does or who she sees.

Later, as Rose is working the front desk, a strange gentleman enters the hotel. Blanche soon enters the lobby, and we learn that the man's name is Tad. Tad is Blanche's mentally retarded brother who lives in an institution in Chattanooga. After some convincing from both Tad and Rose, Blanche allows him to stay for the weekend.

As Chuy and Sophia chat in the kitchen, Chuy asks Sophia about the idea of selling her pizza recipe in order to offer home baked pizza at the Golden Palace. Sophia agrees and makes Chuy promise to never reveal the recipe to anyone. Chuy agrees.

Soon, Rose and Tad are left in the kitchen alone and begin talking. Rose offers to take Tad to the zoo and show him a great time around Miami. Later, Tad tells Blanche that he will not be returning to Chattanooga as he is now in love with Rose.

Sophia teaches Chuy the recipe for the pizza. But, after learning the secret to the pizza, Chuy feels guilty knowing that he only wants to sell the pizza for a profit. Sophia understands, but tells him if he ever reveals the recipe, she'll kill him.

Blanche and Rose have an enormous blowup which ends with Rose stating that Blanche is ashamed of her brother. Surprisingly, Blanche admits that she is embarrassed by Tad.

In the end, Blanche is taking Tad to the bus station. Rose says goodbye and gives a Valentine's Day card to Tad. She explains how special that particular card is. Tad in turn gives it to Blanche. At this point, Blanche indicates that Tad should come to the Golden Palace to visit more often – that way she can show everyone how proud she is of her older brother.

22 - One Angry Stan

Episode Production Number: 23
Filming Location: Hollywood, CA
Original Air Date: April 30, 1993
Episode Length: 24:37
Writer(s): Bill Rosenthal
Director: Lex Passaris

Guest Stars:

Abraham Alvarez (Herb Jenkins)
Earl Boen (The Priest)
Herb Edelman (Stan)
Jennifer Barlow (Bambi)

Episode Description:

The Golden Palace books a bachelor party and is in charge of all the festivities. Even though Rose is not necessarily happy about the idea of a bachelor party, the hotel needs the business. Chuy states he will interview strippers for the show.

The girls anxiously await a visit from Stan's attorney. They are a little put off by the fact that Stan did not come to meet with them himself. That is, until the attorney shows up and informs them that Stan is dead. Rose and Blanche decide that the best way to tell Sophia would be to tell her right before she goes to bed – a plan Rose destroys the second Sophia walks in.

Later, the girls discuss Stan and his will. They all admit that there were times when Stan drove them absolutely crazy. But, they also admit that above all, Stan was a friend and family. As Rose and Blanche leave for the funeral, Sophia stays behind to say a prayer. Just then, Stan walks in and informs Sophia that he faked his death. He must hide from the IRS as he is now broke and a wanted man. After he explains his intents to Sophia, he leaves the hotel.

When a group of women arrive, Roland and Chuy discover that it is not a bachelor party, but rather a bachelorette party. This poses a severe problem because Chuy has booked a woman stripper. The group decides that they would like to see Roland jump out of a cake and strip.

Sophia makes a big scene at the cemetery, continually insisting that Stan is not dead. No one believes her, stating that she is simply grieving. The girls return to the hotel and agree that they must talk to Sophia.

After having gone through what he has, Roland begins to understand how demeaning stripping is. He finds a little compassion for the stripper they had originally hired for the show.

Stan shows up once more to say a final goodbye to Sophia. She tries again to tell him to do the right thing. He refuses, and the two exchange feelings of love for each other. Stan exits. When the girls come back in, Sophia now admits that Stan is gone forever. Stan is now removed from the story line.

23 - Sex, Lies And Tortillas

Episode Production Number: 21
Filming Location: Hollywood, CA
Original Air Date: May 7, 1993
Episode Length: 24:55
Writer(s): Bill Rosenthal, Michael Davidoff
Director: Lex Passaris

Guest Stars:

Micah Dyer (Kid #1)
Robert Cavanaugh (Rick)
Adam Biesk (Benson)
Brooke Theiss (Charlene)
Jep Hill (Kid #2)

Episode Description:

It's spring break time and the hotel is inundated with college-aged guests, in town for a week. Roland is overly concerned about having so many kids in the hotel and consequently, the damage they may cause. After chatting with Chuy about his concerns, the two of them reminisce about their college days. Chuy remembers attempting to build a 43 foot burrito with friends.

Soon, Rose's granddaughter Charlene shows up. But, while Rose has plans for the two of them to see the town together, Charlene actually shows up with her boyfriend. She states she'll be spending time with him.

Concerned about the fact that kids are continually sneaking beer and extra guests into the room, Roland goes undercover trying to catch them in the act. But, almost as soon as he puts on his disguise, he is discovered by the college kids.

Rose is concerned because her granddaughter has expressed an interested in sleeping with her boyfriend – Rose completely disagrees. Charlene eventually leaves and eventually ends up spending the night in another hotel.

Now, a torrential rain comes in, effectively locking all of the kids in the hotel for the rest of the week. Chuy suggests that with all of them locked in, and under the threat of losing all the business, that they make the 43 foot burrito to break the record – everyone agrees.

When Charlene returns from the other hotel, she admits to Rose that she has not yet slept with her boyfriend. Rose decides to finally see her granddaughter as a young woman and not a little girl. Finally, all is well between Rose and her granddaughter.

With the help of all of the college kids staying at the hotel, the burrito is made and Chuy breaks the record. But, soon enough, they need to use the burrito as a sort of dam to save the hotel from being washed away in a flash flood.

24 - The Chicken And The Egg

Episode Production Number: 17
Filming Location: Hollywood, CA
Original Air Date: May 14, 1993
Episode Length: 23:56
Writer(s): Mitchell Hurwitz
Director: Lex Passaris

Guest Stars:

Cynthia Frost (Woman #1)
Reno Goodale (Parking Valet)
Amzie Strickland (Sylvia)
Dick Gautier (Bobby Lee Taggart)
Debra Engle (Rebecca Jean Devereaux)

Episode Description:

As the episode opens, Sophia enters stating that while she was out her car and purse were stolen – although the car in question actually belongs to Rose. Upon hearing how defenseless Sophia was, Roland offers to teach her and her friends self-defense procedures. Unbeknownst to the rest of the group, Roland is actually a blue belt in Martial arts.

It's Blanche's birthday, and as a treat her daughter Rebecca is coming to the Golden Palace for a visit. Although Blanche is excited about her daughter's visit, her usual fears of getting older begins to show through.

Blanche is currently dating a man named Booby Lee, a cattle rancher from Texas. Bobby Lee proposes to Blanche and tells her that along with her hand in marriage, he wants her to have his kids. Even though Blanche has long since passed menopause, she agrees to both of Bobby's proposals. When Blanche shares her ideas with the rest of the staff, they all agree that Blanche's plan has to do with the fact that she is terrified of getting older.

The self-defense course begins with Roland as a teacher. Chuy helps out with the demonstration and bursts into the room as the attacker.

Blanche has now decided that she will ask Rebecca for one of her eggs. Even though Becky really doesn't like the idea, she does finally concede to Blanche – she states that Blanche knows what she wants and will not stand in the way of her plans.

During a dream, Blanche envisions that everyone at the Golden Palace is pregnant – everyone including Roland and Chuy. The dream ends up further confusing Blanche as to her dilemma.

In the end, Blanche's issues are solved for her when she learns that Bobby Lee is sterile. He wants his own children and will not adopt.

It turns out that Sophia's car was not stolen at all. In fact, she actually gave it to the valet at the hotel next door. Her purse, as well as the car is now recovered.

The Closure of *The Golden Palace*

Late in the season, *The Golden Palace* was cancelled due to poor ratings and was not slated for return the following fall. Lackluster ratings are almost always the reason a young show is cancelled after just one season. Obviously, ratings are the most important parts of the decision making process network executives go through when deciding if a show will remain on the air.

As a part of writing this book, interviews were conducted regarding the show as a whole, and I have compiled the results. The most frequent opinions of those who were asked about the show's failure pointed to the departure of Bea Arthur. After the conclusion of *The Golden Girls,* the remaining three girls attempted to keep the laughs going, and while they were successful, the original magic was never there again. Just as some missed Dorothy with enough prejudice to not watch *The Golden Palace,* some never adjusted to the new cast members. The fact is, most people seem to look at *The Golden Palace* as an eighth season to *The Golden Girls,* which it simply is not. Even though 75% of the cast would move to a Miami Beach hotel, the cast of *The Golden Palace* was not that of *The Golden Girls.* Plenty of folks never adjusted to the new cast trying to fit into the lives of their beloved golden girls.

So how does the show now fit into the world of *The Golden Girls?* Simply put, there is a major difference in how people look at *The Golden Palace* then and now. In the fall of 1992, hardcore fans tuned in and hoped that they would be able to continue the laughs with a new show. A majority of these fans soon fell off the bandwagon and found another show to invest their laughs into. The show simply was not the original idea with the original cast. But, now that we have been without the girls altogether for over 16 years, *The Golden Palace* takes on a different appeal. Now, it's our obsession with the characters themselves that brings us in. There are no more episodes of *The Golden Girls*, and there never will be. So, we use *The Golden Palace* as a way to get a little more out of our favorite television characters. After all, Dorothy, Stan and Miles all appear in episodes in order to keep the ties to the original show strong.

So, after just a single season *The Golden Palace* would fall into television history. It seems sad that nowadays so many people make comments about how humorous and well written the stories were. But, let's not forget that the poor viewership was the reason the show was cancelled in the first place. Had more people tuned in to witness the craziness of the staff of *The Golden Palace,* a second season may have been in the works at some point. At the very least, we have 24 episodes to hold in our hearts forever.

GOOFS, NOTES AND OBSERVATIONS
The Golden Palace

This section can often be one of the most fun parts of any viewing guide. This is where the reality of life and the magic of a television show come together. Complied from research and from my own observations, this is a short list of "goofs," notes and observations about the show *The Golden Palace*. While admittedly a short list due to the single-season status of the show, use this section as a way to enjoy the show on a whole new level.

Episode #1 - *The Pilot - (The Golden Palace)*

With the departure of Bea Arthur, the cast billing sequence changes. Now, Betty White is top-billed. How popular a star is usually has to do with the order in which they come up on the screen during opening credits. Of course, their agent and the contract they signed have just as much to do with the order they appear as anything else.

The old set from *The Golden Girls* is utilized for one last time. Although we know it is the same house, it certainly looks a bit odd with only one piece of furniture left and papers scattered everywhere. But, it was a great way to close out *The Golden Girls,* and begin the short life of *The Golden Palace.*

The theme song utilizes the same lyrics and the same name, "Thank you for being a friend." This version is more upbeat and sung by a man, and is sometimes referred to as the "reggae" mix.

Here, we meet the new cast members – Don Cheadle as Roland Wilson, the current hotel manager. Cheech Marin, from the famous Cheech and Chong duo, steps into a role as Chuy, the hotel cook. Finally, newcomer Billy L. Sullivan rounds out the cast as Oliver. However, the character of Oliver is dicey at best and only appears in a few episodes – 1 through 6 and 14.

The Golden Palace was created by the famed Susan Harris – however, as is sometimes the fate of spin-offs, it failed after a very short life.

Episode #2 - *Promotional Considerations*

This episode deals with a constantly recurring problem on the show – Blanche's power trip and desire to always be in control. This was never really an issue on *The Golden Girls,* with Blanche often being shown as a helpless woman clearly in need of friends. Here, in *The Golden Palace,* Blanche continually ends up in power struggles with the other staff members, although as shown here, usually with Roland.

The theme music used for *The Barbara LaGrange Show* is the same music that was used in *The Golden Girls* episode titled: "Grab that dough!" While some may maintain this was done intentionally to show a connection between the two shows, more than likely that's not the truth. Often, when in the need of items like the show them music, it's sometimes easier to simply use the same track they already have on hand.

This episode features comic veteran Bobcat Goldthwait. His crazy voice and erratic behavior make him the perfect actor for the character being played – a man the girls are convinced is a killer staying at the hotel.

Episode #3 - *Miles, We Hardly Knew Ye*

Probably means nothing in the grand scheme of things, but it should be noted that the hotel guest registry goes back to 1985. It almost seems that this is intentional considering 1985 is when *The Golden Girls* first premiered.

Here, Harold Gould makes a cross-over appearance from *The Golden Girls* as the character Miles Weber. By the end of the episode, Miles will admit that there is another woman in his life and will leave Rose. However, he will return briefly in a later episode.

Chuy makes a statement that he learned about the infidelity of his wife by reading about it in graffiti. But, in a later episode, "Ebbtide for the Defense," Chuy states that he discovered his best friend Rubin in bed with her. It is kind of odd to find this type of "goof" with two episodes so close to each other in the same season.

Episode #4 - *One Old Lady To Go*

In this episode, we see a lot of "side info" about the characters of the show. Most notably Sophia reveals that she can, and does, remove bottle caps with her teeth. We also learn that Rose spent 7 years working on a Rubik's cube - again, interesting to hear the number 7 as that would point to the exact time when *The Golden Girls* began. We also learn that Roland enjoys playing the piano.

The idea Sophia has for the Chinese food delivery is very reminiscent of the many ideas the girls had for money making scams in *The Golden Girls.* Most of the ideas they have had were depicted in the episode "One for the Money." As with other attempts to make a quick buck, the Chinese food idea doesn't fly and by the end of the episode, the idea is buried.

Two cross-over from other shows should be mentioned. First, Anne Haney had previously played a character on Mama's family – a show which also starred Betty White and Rue McClanahan. Here Anne plays a character named Vivian. Anne also appeared in an episode of *The Golden Girls* as Dorothy's hospital roommate.

Episode #5 - *Ebbtide For The Defense*

The word "Ebbtide" seems to be a favorite of either the writers, the producers or the creator of the show – whoever names the episodes. This is the fourth time the word comes up in the span of the two shows. "Ebbtide" shows up three times in *The Golden Girls* titles, and now with this episode.

The man who plays Rubin, Gregory Sierra, has had recurring roles on both the shows *Soap* and

Nurses. Both of these shows were created by Susan Harris. Of course, producers and creators sometimes use the same actors from show to show.

Episode #6 - *Can't Stand Losing You*

Kim Fields guest stars as Roland's ex-girlfriend Trish. In 1992, Kim made two separate acting appearances in an attempt to break away from her former role on *The Facts of Life.* Her appearance on this episode of *The Golden Palace* was her first attempt at that goal.

Blanche admits to having once had an affair with Jerry Lee Lewis. At that point, Rose chimes in and admits to a former affair with Mayor McCheese. In the old MacDonald's restaurant commercials, Mayor McCheese was a well known character.

This is Billy Sullivan's second to last appearance. He disappears from now on until the episode titled "Runaways" where he is reclaimed by his foster mother. After this episode, Billy is removed from the opening credits until the "Runaways" episode.

Episode #7 - *Seems Like Old Times (Part 1)*

Ah! Finally the girls are reunited again. This is part one of a two part episode featuring Bea Arthur. These two episodes were the most viewed and highest rated of the entire season of *The Golden Palace.* It was painfully obvious that America missed the old cast being together and when Bea appeared, the ratings shot through the roof. Unfortunately, after these two episodes, the ratings would fall back again.

As the cast is again united, we see the infamous group hug the girls were constantly engaged in on *The Golden Girls.* The love for each other is as strong as ever, but eventually problems would surface that would require the girls to remember the friendship they formed so long ago.

This is the first episode which has no mention, nor appearance of Oliver. Billy Sullivan disappears from the credits and will not reappear until episode number 14, titled "Runaways."

Episode #8 - *Seems Like Old Times (Part 2)*

In this episode, we finally get to see the infamous Shady Pines, a carry-over from *The Golden Girls.* The fire and destruction of Shady Pines became the very reason Sophia came to live with the girls in the beginning. Sophia always had described the retirement home as a living hell. But, we get to see how Shady Pines really is. Apparently, the home is the definition of luxury living for retirees. Dorothy and the other girls arrive at the home to take Sophia back to the Golden Palace.

This is the final time the four characters will ever be seen in their former roles from *The Golden Girls.* As Bea Arthur walks off the set in the final scene, her character is all but a memory.

Upon preparing to leave the Golden Palace, Dorothy is presented with a lifetime membership to the hotel. They indicate that no matter what happens or how far they are apart, Dorothy is always a part of them.

It is kind of an oddity, but after the girls tell Dorothy that she is always welcome and she is always a part of them, they suddenly all end up busy with different hotel tasks. As such, Dorothy is left to walk out of the hotel alone. It almost seems to drive a wedge which says that they are all still friends, but their lives are now totally separate and very different.

Episode #9 - *Just A Gigolo*

This episode has an interesting tie to *The Golden Girls.* This is the second time a conman pulls Blanche in to a steamy romance with the intention of simply trying to steal from her. We saw this happen late in the original series during a "Moonlight Madness" party. It is Rose who saves Blanche from both conmen in both shows.

The actor who plays Nick, Barry Bostwick, is best known for his work in musical theater as well as for portraying Brad Majors in "The Rocky Horror Picture Show." He is a very accomplished actor and wanted to branch into television. *The Golden Palace* was one of his first stops in the world of television.

In revealing more of her past, Blanche shares that she was once slapped with a sexual harassment lawsuit after she licked a gardener's neck. This is only one of many legal troubles Blanche admits to which are directly related to her over-active sex drive.

Episode #10 - *Marriage On The Rocks, With A Twist*

Yet again, Sophia ends up involved in a long running practical joke where Rose is the target. This is reminiscent of a few situations portrayed or explained on *The Golden Girls.* But, as we see in the end, Rose has fun making sure that on this round, Sophia gets her turn to be the fool and the victim of the joke.

Both Betty White and Rue McClanahan are reunited with Harvey Korman. The three stared on the show *Mama's Family* together.

We also see the classic teamwork of Harvey Korman and Tim Conway. These two came to work together and form a famous comic partnership on the live action skit television beacon, *The Carol Burnett Show.*

Episode #11 - *Camp Town Races Aren't Nearly As Much Fun As They Used To Be*

Blanche is yet again associated with an organization paying tribute to the old South. In *The Golden Girls,* Blanche tried to get accepted into The Daughters of the Confederacy. Here, The Daughters of the Traditional South are coming to stay at the hotel.

Although Blanche does not try to gain entrance to this club, she does continually make comments and add decoration to the hotel that offends Roland. After her run in with the Daughters of the Confederacy in the past, it seems very odd that she would even mildly entertain any association with a group like this.

Rose is extremely upset by the fact that an apparent extramarital affair is going on at the hotel. Her reaction seems a bit extreme for a woman who was involved in an affair herself in *The Golden Girls* episode "In a Bed of Rose's."

Episode #12 - *It's Beginning To Look a Lot (Less) Like Christmas*

In this episode, the Charles Dickens classic tale, "A Christmas Carol" is referenced when Chuy is visited by three Christmas ghosts. Notice how the second is the ghost of "Christmas presents." Dickens's tale is referenced often during Christmas time, but the application of the staff of the Golden Palace makes this one very special and humorous.

The placement of set items moves in this episode. The freezer has moved to a different location – in other episodes it ends up outside the kitchen, here it is in the room. Also, Chuy is seen many times as going upstairs to his room, indicating that he keeps a room in the hotel as his quarters. But, Blanche makes references to Chuy's room being outside and more behind the hotel. Obviously, the latter would make more sense as the last thing a hotel would do is give up usable guest rooms.

Episode #13 - *Rose And Fern*

Here, we learn that Rose has had a nickel stuck in her head since she was a child, possibly explaining her odd behavior. Apparently, the nickel got stuck as a result of a magic trick which went horribly wrong.

We also hear that Rose had initially wanted to have a cow-themed wedding, a popular option in her hometown of St. Olaf. However, Rose explains that this would eventually become a non-option, as Charlie was lactose intolerant.

In what was definitely an odd maneuver for Rose, we discover that she has been making harassing phone calls to Miles. Apparently, Rose never completely got over the loss of Miles. But, as the episode closes, we see Rose witnessing Miles marry Fern, his fiancé. Rose states this is the only way she will have closure and be able to move on.

This is the second and final appearance of Harold Gould playing Miles in the series. After this episode, Miles is never seen or referenced again.

Episode #14 - *Runaways*

A recurring them spilled over from *The Golden Girls* is Sophia's constant obsession with her desire to drive. Everyone around her is always adamant about keeping her from being behind the wheel, but she always seems to succeed. Here, she steals a car, and the soon to be departed Oliver, and heads out to the open road.

This is the final episode to feature Billy Sullivan as Oliver. While has was inexplicably missing for several episodes beforehand, he is suddenly brought back. At this point, his mother, recovered from a drug addiction, returns to reclaim him. Obviously Roland, Oliver's foster parent is the most affected by the loss. Oliver is never mentioned again in the show.

Episode #15 - *Heartbreak Hotel*

While it may mean absolutely nothing, there are some fans who make a connection to Blanche's obsession with Elvis from *The Golden Girls* and the title of the episode. "Heartbreak Hotel" was a hit single from Elvis in the mid 1950's.

Blanche states having some issues with the man from her past featured here, Taylor, played by Dick Van Patten. Blanche's concern with Taylor seems a bit odd as she paints him as the only man she was not able to conquer. However, in *The Golden Girls,* she states to have had issues with another man, Ham Lushbaum.

There is another connection which at the time of the show was yet to be made. Dick Van Patten and Betty White would appear on another show to hit the airwaves in 1995 called *Maybe This Time.*

Episode #16 - *Señor Stinky Learns Absolutely Nothing About Life*

This is the one and only episode of *The Golden Girls* and *The Golden Palace* which has the other cast members concerned about Blanche's sexual advances. Blanche actually learns that she is running a business and has responsibilities. This is an amazing plot twist as this has never been addressed anywhere in either of the shows.

Stephen James Carver reprises the role of Brad, the pool man, who previously appeared in the "Pilot" episode. Brad is the only other hotel staff member who appears in more than one episode.

Ricardo Montalban, a veteran actor, plays the suave hotel owner Mr. Gentry. He ends up being a big challenge for Blanche as she attempts to keep from mixing business with pleasure.

Episode #17 - *Say Goodbye, Rose*

Here, we learn that Sophia took on a rather interesting project while living in Brooklyn in the 1950's. Apparently she recorded a very raunchy comedy album under the false name "Ma Petrillo." There is no mention of Sophia's, apparently short lived, comedy career in *The Golden Girls.*

Following the above premise, Sophia admits that she knows "over one thousand Blanche slut jokes." As we know, this is a carryover from *The Golden Girls.* Of course, all of the girls take stabs at Blanche for her promiscuity during the course of the two shows, but obviously Sophia is well above the others in hitting her mark.

We also learn yet another off fact about the colorful people of St. Olaf. According to Rose, people in St.Olaf dance on their heads.

It's a little confusing to think that George had to work at a carnival to put himself through college. We have heard many references to the wealth of George's family in several episodes. So, it seems a bit odd that he would need such a job.

Episode #18 - *You've Lost That Living Feeling*

Some viewers find it odd that the lobby would be decorated with balloons and such the day before the arrival of Mr. Davenport. It seems that at the very least the balloons would be a last minute addition due to their tendency to lose helium after several hours.

Most television shows have at least one sub-plot going on at the same time as the main plot. Generally, this is to keep the interest of the audience and to add some comedic relief. Basically, a secondary plot is added to ease the tension on the main plot. In this particular episode, there is no secondary plot. The whole idea of the episode has to do with the food critic's death and the staff reacting to the problems arising from it.

Not a goof, but rather a television error of interest. When this episode aired on Lifetime Television, the scene with Sophia and Chuy removing the body from the laundry chute was actually shown *after* the closing credits.

Episode 19 – *A New Leash on Life*

Due to the interests of Betty White and Rue McClanahan, we see this episode come up dealing with racing dogs. The character of Rose is extremely concerned about the possibility of a dog being euthanized. Both Rue and Betty took a special interest in the subject matter of this episode.

Ken Kercheval is better known for his 1980's appearance in the nighttime soap *Dallas.* Mr. Kercheval portrayed the arch enemy Cliff Barnes.

Ja'net DuBois is also known for another role as well. Most will remember her from the hit 1970's sit-com *Good Times.*

Episode 20 – *Pro and Concierge*

This episode is important as it finally shows Roland leaving the Golden Palace, albeit only for a portion of the episode. But, Roland talks several times during the series about leaving and even though Blanche asks him to leave, he actually does go.

Episode 21 – *Tad*

The majority of the cast says "Chattanooga" incorrectly. The correct pronunciation for the town in "CHATTAnooga".

Ned Beatty guest stars. Ned also had major roles in "Deliverance," and of course, as Dan's father on television's *Rosanne*.

It seems odd that after eight years, we finally get to hear of Blanche's brother. Even though she is apparently embarrassed by his condition, it's still shocking to go this long with no mention of him previously.

Episode 22 – *One Angry Stan*

This is the final appearance of Stan. Here, the entire rest of the staff will become convinced that Stan is gone. Only Sophia will know the truth – that Stan has gone to Madrid to hide from the I.R.S. Herb Edelman, who played Stan, would be the first member of the cast to pass away just a few years later.

Here we learn that, thanks to Stan, Sophia had plastic surgery on her neck. She mentions this several times throughout the episode and is apparently quite proud of having the work done.

Blanche mentions the fact that bald men seem to have a thing for her, which she doesn't seem to mind very much. In fact, she mentions having had several bad men between her cleavage. But, in *The Golden Girls,* she mentions being terrified of bald men.

Episode 23 – *Sex, Lies and Tortillas*

Here we meet Rose's granddaughter Charlene. There is a large belief that the woman who played Charlene is the same person who played her granddaughter Charlie in the first season of *The Golden Girls.* This is a common misconception and is not true.

Here we lean about both Roland and Chuy's younger days. Roland explains some of the younger portions of his life including college and his fraternity days. Meanwhile Chuy explains how he and his old friends tried to break the record for the longest burrito. While Chuy states that a much shorter burrito would break the record, in reality, the current record for the longest burrito is just over 8400ft.

Episode 24 – *The Chicken and the Egg*

Sophia mentions having had a purse for 30 years. There is no way this is true as in *The Golden Girls,* she states that her purse shrunk down to a change purse after she had tried to recover Preparation H from the floor.

Here we see crossover character from *The Golden Girls.* Rebecca, Blanche's daughter, comes back and almost ends up giving Blanche one of her eggs so that Blanche may have a baby.

At this point, it would be difficult, if not impossible, considering she went through menopause during the second season. This occurred six years before this episode aired.

The Golden Palace
Trivia Challenge!

Ready to test your knowledge about *The Golden Palace?* On the following pages, you will find 100 random difficulty questions about one of the funniest, albeit short lived, sitcoms to ever exist! The questions are multiple choice, true or false, and fill in the blank. Challenge yourself, challenge your friends!

Answers are provided in an answer key following the end of the trivia section.

Good Luck!

1. **What is the first name of Oliver's mother?**

A. Rebecca
B. Jenna
C. Susan
D. Paula

2. **Rose discovers that Miles is involved with another woman. What was her name?**

A. Betty
B. Gladys
C. Fern
D. Mildred

3. **True or False: The first episode of The Golden Palace shows the girls moving out?**

A. True
B. False

4. **What is the name of the two part episode starring Bea Arthur as Dorothy?**

A. Friends Again!
B. Seems Like Old Times
C. How Long Has It Been?
D. Reunited!

5. **What is the name of the hotel pool boy?**

A. Brad
B. Marcus
C. Tommy
D. Bill

6. **What name did an adulterous couple check in under that caused high anxiety for Rose?**

A. Mr. and Mrs. Nylund
B. Mr. and Mrs. Don Schula
C. Mr. and Mrs. Jones
D. Mr. and Mrs. Smith

7. **What is the name of the mentally challenged brother of Blanche's we meet late in the season?**

A. Phil
B. Andrew
C. David
D. Tad

8. *Which member of The Golden Palace crew decides to start a lost and found box for extra income?*

A. Rose
B. Oliver
C. Sophia
D. Roland

9. *True or False: Rose hyperventilates during the pilot episode after seeing a mouse in the hotel?*

A. True
B. False

10. *Chuy tries out his stand-up comedy under what stage name?*

A. Chuy the cut-up
B. Chuy, the Mexican comedian
C. Chuy, the Mexican chef
D. Corny Costillos

11. *What was the name of Chuy's ex friend who he caught in bed with is wife?*

A. Marcus
B. Hector
C. Philip
D. Rubin

12. *What city did Chuy grow up in?*

A. Miami
B. Portland
C. Dallas
D. Los Angeles

13. *Does Chuy get remarried during the series?*

A. Yes
B. No

14. *What is the name of the Alzheimer stricken woman rose befriends who stays at the hotel?*

A. Janet
B. Barbara
C. Geri
D. Vivian

15. _**Blanche's son Matthew comes for a visit. What is the news he has for his mother?**_

A. He has received a tattoo
B. He has quit his job
C. He is moving in with his girlfriend
D. He is gay

16. _**What is the news Blanche thinks her son has for her?**_

A. He has quit his job
B. He is moving to another country
C. He is getting married
D. He is gay

17. _**In Ebbtide for the defense, what two groups of people were guests at the hotel?**_

A. Judges and lawyers
B. Lawyers and a motorcycle gang
C. Clowns and Firemen
D. Casino owners and bankers

18. _**What is directly behind the front desk in the lobby of the hotel?**_

A. Mailboxes
B. A bulletin board
C. A window to the kitchen
D. Chuy's room

19. _**What does Chuy decide to use to describe the birds and the bees to Oliver?**_

A. Action figures
B. A drawing
C. Puppets
D. A story from his past

20. _**What items that Blanche orders show up with an embarrassing misprint?**_

A. Pens
B. Pencils
C. T Shirts
D. Pins

21. _**Where was The Golden Palace taped?**_

A. Hollywood Studios
B. Ren-Mar Studios
C. Sunset Gower Studios
D. Riva Studios

22. *__What is the name of the hotel Roland tried to get a job at after being fired?__*

A. Holiday Inn
B. The Renaissance
C. The Manor
D. The Carlton

23. *__Who fires Roland causing him to look for a new job?__*

A. Rose
B. Blanche
C. Sophia
D. Chuy

24. *__Which local show wanted Chuy to appear and cook on stage?__*

A. *Say Hello Miami*
B. *Wake Up Miami*
C. *Good Morning America*
D. *The Florida Edition*

25. *__What is the most prevalent problem featured at The Golden Palace?__*

A. Not enough employees
B. Not enough guests
C. Not enough restaurant business
D. Not enough towels

26. *__True or False: Roland welcomes the girls with open arms when the first walk in?__*

A. True
B. False

27. *__How many employees does the hotel have when the girls first take ownership?__*

A. Thirty Five
B. Eleven
C. Twenty Two
D. Three

28. *__What is the name of the famed restaurant critic who visits the hotel?__*

A. Gerald Davenport
B. Philip Reinhardt
C. Samuel Dunham
D. William Powell

29. *In "Ebbtide for the Defense," what does the hotel "lose" that concerns Roland?*

A.   Their hotel liability insurance
B.   Their business permits
C.   Their tax records
D.   Their license to run a restaurant

30. *Who was the creator of The Golden Palace?*

A.   Margaret Whitney
B.   Susan Reilly
C.   Susan Harris
D.   Angela Lakes

31. *What do Blanche and Roland use to discover that Miles is cheating?*

A.   Old hotel guest books
B.   Photos from an old hotel function
C.   An admittance from another hotel guest
D.   An old love letter they find

32. *Who does Chuy hit on when she walks into The Golden Palace after his divorce?*

A.   Dorothy
B.   Rose
C.   Sophia
D.   A hotel guest named Renee

33. *True or False: Shady Pines was nothing like the descriptions Sophia had always given?*

A.   True
B.   False

34. *What was Sophia receiving from an orderly when the girls arrive at Shady Pines?*

A.   A massage
B.   A foot-rub
C.   A manicure
D.   A pedicure

35. *What is the name of the gigolo in the episode "Just a gigolo?"*

A.   Andrew
B.   Nick
C.   Dave
D.   Eric

36. *What is Rose's granddaughter's name?*

A.   Rebecca
B.   Charlene
C.   Rachel
D.   Dana

37. *What was the name of the women's group staying at the hotel that Roland objected to?*

A.   The Sisters of the South
B.   The Ladies of Southern Pride
C.   The Daughters of the Traditional South
D.   The Atlanta League of Women

38. *What are the names of the two radio hosts who appeared at The Golden Palace?*

A.   Bill and Andrew
B.   Tim and Tom
C.   Eric and Dave
D.   Bill and Milton

39. *How long did it take Rose to solve a Rubik's Cube?*

A.   Five years
B.   Six years
C.   Seven years
D.   3 months

40. *Whose parents show up and announce a divorce?*

A.   Roland's
B.   Chuy's
C.   Oliver's
D.   Blanche's

41. *According to an episode, what sport is Chuy very bad at playing?*

A.   Volleyball
B.   Baseball
C.   Softball
D.   Basketball

42. *True or False: Betty White is an animal activist?*

A.   True
B.   False

43. ***Who is Jim Vallely?***

A. A guest star on The Golden Palace
B. A director from The Golden Place
C. A writer from The Golden Palace
D. A character's name

44. ***Who is Lex Passaris?***

A. A guest star on The Golden Palace
B. A director from The Golden Palace
C. A writer from The Golden Palace
D. A character's name

45. ***What talk show does The Golden Palace act as an official hotel for?***

A. The Oprah Winfrey Show
B. The Tim Fields Show
C. The Barbara LaGrange Show
D. The Bill Miles Show

46. ***Whose idea was it to offer the hotel for promotional reasons to the above show?***

A. Rose
B. Blanche
C. Oliver
D. Chuy

47. ***What date did the pilot episode air?***

A. September 18, 1992
B. October 7, 1992
C. September 8, 1992
D. September 1, 1992

48. ***Blanche ruins a business appointment by flirting with the man she is meeting with. He is:***

A. A banker
B. A pool technician
C. A furniture representative
D. A contractor

49. ***In the final episode, what is Blanche trying to get Rebecca to donate?***

A. Money
B. An egg
C. A car
D. A house

50. *When Roland is fired from The Golden Palace, where does he finally find a job?*

A. A convenience store
B. A bike rental shop
C. A bus terminal
D. A train station

51. *What is the name of Blanche's mentally retarded brother?*

A. Tad
B. Ted
C. Fred
D. Ned

52. *Where does Blanche's mentally retarded brother reside?*

A. Chattanooga
B. Memphis
C. Dallas
D. Atlanta

53. *In the Christmas episode, who plays the ghost of Christmas past?*

A. Rose
B. Roland
C. Sophia
D. Blanche

54. *Who is the ghost of Christmas presents?*

A. Rose
B. Sophia
C. Blanche
D. Roland

55. *And finally the ghost of Christmas yet to come is?*

A. Rose
B. Sophia
C. Oliver
D. Roland

56. *Who, in the Christmas episode, asks that decorations be taken down?*

A. The leader of a support group
B. The local police chief
C. The mayor of Miami
D. Roland

57. *The use of what drug is made reference to regarding Chuy's past?*

A. Caffeine
B. Marijuana
C. Cocaine
D. Painkillers

58. *True or False: Cheech Marin was once part of a famous comedy trio?*

A. True
B. False

59. *Who is the first character from The Golden Girls to cross over into The Golden Palace?*

A. Miles
B. Stan
C. Dorothy
D. Dr. Harry Westin

60. *In the episode "Promotional Considerations," what is Sophia's promotional idea?*

A. Handing out fliers for margaritas
B. Handing out pens to promote The Golden Place
C. T-shirts with a crazy Italian slogan
D. Pins that say: "The Golden Palace is the place to be!"

61. *Who plays the crazy hotel guest in the same episode?*

A. Don Knotts
B. Bobcat Goldthwait
C. George Carlin
D. Tommy Chong

62. *When Rose finds a date for Roland, what is her name?*

A. Madge
B. Megan
C. Joanne
D. Denise

63. *Who was the "embezzler" from the hotel?*

A. Blanche
B. Roland
C. Rose
D. Oliver

64. **What recurring phrase does Dorothy use when she visits the hotel?**

A.   Walk away now and no one gets hurt
B.   Leave me alone and I won't hurt you
C.   I don't know what you're talking about
D.   I'm rich and you can't tell me no

65. **What game show does Sophia want to travel to Los Angeles to compete on?**

A.   *Jeopardy!*
B.   *Grab that dough!*
C.   *The price is right*
D.   *Wheel of fortune*

66. **Who is the last cross-over character from The Golden Girls to appear?**

A.   Dorothy
B.   Dr. Harry Westin
C.   Stan
D.   Miles

67. **In the episode "Say goodbye Rose," what is the name of the man Rose falls for?**

A.   Bill
B.   Phil
C.   Bobby
D.   Joseph

68. **Why does Rose fall for the man mentioned in question #67?**

A.   He resembles Charlie
B.   He is a doctor
C.   He is a veterinarian
D.   He is a chef

69. **What kitchen appliance needs to be repaired at the start of "Rose and Fern?"**

A.   The sink
B.   An industrial blender
C.   The oven
D.   The lights

70. **According to an episode title, who is "Senor Stinky?"**

A.   Roland
B.   Chuy
C.   Oliver
D.   Blanche

71. *What is Stan's latest scheme in the episode "One angry Stan?"*

A. He invents a new baked potato opener.
B. He invents a new type of toupee glue
C. He fakes his own death
D. He cheats on his current wife and blames it on Sophia

72. *Who is the only member of The Golden Palace staff to know the truth about Stan?*

A. Sophia
B. Oliver
C. Blanche
D. Chuy

73. *What was Sophia's husband's name?*

A. Salvatore
B. Guido
C. Angelo
D. Miliban

74. *Who dies in the hotel prompting the staff to hide the body?*

A. A food critic
B. A hotel critic
C. A health inspector
D. An oven repairman

75. *The hotel holds a sweet sixteen party. Whose daughter is turning 16?*

A. The hotels banker
B. Sophia's friend
C. The hotel's pool boy Brad
D. Blanche's sister Virginia

76. *What are the two accusations the visiting radio hosts make about Blanche?*

A. She is gay and a bad dresser
B. She is a transvestite and a transsexual
C. She is a bad cook and housekeeper
D. She is a virgin and is ugly

77. *Why does Blanche end up on a date with a gigolo?*

A. Her date cancels
B. Her date tells her he over slept
C. Her date dies
D. She decides she likes the gigolo better than her date.

78. ***In the final episode, what crazy dream does Blanche have?***

A. She is now the owner of the hotel as the entire staff his quit
B. The entire staff has won a huge amount of money in a lottery
C. The entire staff is pregnant
D. The entire staff has turned gay

79. ***Which episode was the highest rated by television viewers?***

A. One angry Stan
B. Seems like old times
C. The Golden Palace (the pilot)
D. The Sophia who knew too much

80. ***Name all of Dorothy's siblings***

A. _____

B. _____

81. ***What is the name of Blanche's gay brother?***

A. Clayton
B. Philip
C. Jeffrey
D. William

82. ***What is the name of the house Blanche grew up in?***

A. Hewings House
B. Hollingsworth Manner
C. Hollingsworth House
D. The Hollingsworth Estate

83. ***What type of food does Sophia begin making to make extra money?***

A. Chinese
B. Italian
C. Greek
D. Mediterranean

84. ***What was the name of the restaurant Sophia was stealing business from?***

A. The Golden Carole
B. The Golden Palace
C. The Red Fox
D. The Golden Cat

85. *Blanche actually is referred to by two middle names throughout the years. What are they?*

A. Marie and Elizabeth
B. Gretchen and Mary
C. Kelly and Susan
D. Marie and Mary

86. *Who was top billed in the credits during The Golden Girls?*

A. Bea Arthur
B. Estelle Getty
C. Betty White
D. Rue McClanahan

87. *Who took the top billing spot in The Golden Palace?*

A. Cheech Marin
B. Betty White
C. Estelle Getty
D. Don Cheadle

88. *Who does Roland become convinced his mom is fooling around with?*

A. Chuy
B. Mr. Garcia from the neighboring hotel
C. Mr. Swanza from the local convenience store
D. Sophia

89. *What does Sophia state is her main purpose in life, at The Golden Palace?*

A. To cook 50 different kinds of food every day
B. To cook 50 lbs. of ravioli every day
C. To cook Mexican, American and Italian food
D. To keep the customers happy

90. *What is Blanche's primary job at the hotel?*

A. Working the front desk
B. Running the kitchen
C. Running the dining room
D. Housekeeping

91. *What is Rose's primary job at the hotel?*

A. Working the front desk
B. Running the kitchen
C. Running the dining room
D. Housekeeping

92.   *What is Sophia's primary job at the hotel?*

A.   Helping Chuy in the kitchen
B.   Being a co-chef with Chuy in the kitchen
C.   Running the front desk
D.   Drumming up more guests

93.   *What year do the guest books go back to in episode #2*

A.   1981
B.   1962
C.   1972
D.   1985

94.   *What is interesting about the year the hotel books go back to?*

A.   It was during the Korean War
B.   It was the year The Golden Girls began
C.   It was the year the creator of the show was born
D.   It was the year Miles met Rose

95.   *Harold Gould played another part on The Golden Girls during season #1?*

A.   Philip
B.   Robert
C.   Joseph
D.   Arnie

96.   *What is the classic story beginning that follows from The Golden Girls?*

A.   Picture it, Sicily
B.   When I was young in Italy
C.   Picture it, I was a young Italian
D.   Back in Sicily

97.   *Roland states that he does not kill bugs. What does he do?*

A.   He "shoes them"
B.   He "squishes them"
C.   He "serenades them"
D.   He "scares them"

98.   *What dead animal does Roland refuse to touch in the kitchen?*

A.   Beef
B.   Chicken
C.   Lamb
D.   Pork

99. ***What is the name of the woman Chuy marries in the episode "Seems like old times?"***

A. Mary
B. Melissa
C. Sabrina
D. Beverly

100. ***What is the problem with Chuy's new bride?***

A. She will not consummate the marriage
B. She is controlling
C. She is never around
D. She does not like the rest of the staff.

The Golden Palace
Trivia Challenge!

-The Answer Key-

1. Paula

2. Fern

3. True

4. Seems Like Old Times

5. Brad

6. Mr. and Mrs. Smith

7. Tad

8. Oliver

9. False

10. Corny Costillos

11. Rubin

12. Los Angeles

13. No

14. Vivian

15. He has quit his job

16. He is gay

17. Lawyers and a motorcycle gang

18. Mailboxes

19. Puppets

20. Pens

21. Ren Mar Studios

22. The Carlton

23. Blanche

24. *Wake Up Miami*

25. Not enough guests

26. False

27. Three

28. Gerald Davenport

29. Their hotel liability insurance

30. Susan Harris

31. Old hotel guest books

32. Dorothy

33. True

34. A massage

35. Nick

36. Charlene

37. The Daughters of the Traditional South

38. Bill and Milton

39. Seven years

40. Roland's

41. Volleyball

42. True

43. A writer from *The Golden Palace*

44. A director from *The Golden Palace*

45. *The Barbara LaGrange Show*

46. Rose

47. September 18, 1992

48. A banker

49. An egg

50. A bike rental shop

51. Tad

52. Chatanooga

53. Rose

54. Blanche

55. Sophia

56. The leader of a support group

57. Marijuana

58. False

59. Miles

60. Handing out fliers for margaritas

61. Bobcat Goldthwait

62. Joanne

63. Blanche

64. Walk away now and no one gets hurt

65. *The Price is Right*

66. Stan

67. Bill

68. He resembles Charlie

69. The oven

70. Chuy

71. He fakes his own death

72. Sophia

73. Salvatore

74. A food critic

75. The hotel's banker

76. She is a transvestite and a transsexual

77. Her date dies

78. The entire staff is pregnant

79. Seems like old times

80. Phil and Gloria

81. Clayton

82. Hollingsworth Manor

83. Chinese

84. The Golden Palace

85. Marie and Elizabeth

86. Bea Arthur

87. Betty White

88. Chuy

89. To cook 50 lbs. of ravioli every day

90. Working the front desk

91. Housekeeping

92. Being a co-chef with Chuy in the kitchen

93. 1985

94. It was the year *The Golden Girls* began

95. Arnie

96. Picture it, Sicily

97. He "shoes them"

98. Chicken

99. Beverly

100. She will not consummate the marriage

Where can I still watch *The Golden Palace?*

As with any television show, our most prevalent desire is to be able to watch our favorite episodes over and over again, whenever we desire. With the advent of DVD technology, this dream became much more attainable. We have witnessed all seven seasons of *The Golden Girls* released on DVD and now we can see full uninterrupted episodes whenever we want.

But, unfortunately, *The Golden Palace* is a bit of a different issue. Many people consider *The Golden Palace* to be another season of *The Golden Girls,* sans one character. But, that's not the way production companies and studio heads see the show. In their eyes, the show was a flop. It only lasted one season and 24 episodes. As you may be aware, it normally takes many more episodes to allow a show to go into syndication and eventually be released on DVD.

Being that only 24 episodes exist, it was remarkable that Lifetime Television was able to work a deal to show them. If you had the chance to catch the episodes, you got to relive the amazing moments with the cast of *The Golden Palace.* But, the run of the show only lasted for a few days and then was again returned to the vault. A remarkable amount of effort and money was put into having that short run on Lifetime. It is unlikely that it will happen again on that station or another for that matter.

So, does this mean that it will never be available again? In short, no. There is a very good possibility that if enough interest is shown by the general public, it may eventually be released on video. However, there is also a very good possibility that as we get further away from 1992, that it may never become a reality. Internet petitions may help to push the show onto DVD, but the expense involved continues to push it back down.

There are ways to see the show though, namely through the Internet and video sites such as YouTube. The entire series is available for viewing, whenever you want, just by logging on to that site.

The Golden Girls and *The Golden Palace* may be gone forever, but at least in the case of the original show, there is always DVD. However, *The Golden Palace* may very well remain a show you'll need to search for on the Internet to watch.

Printed in Great Britain
by Amazon